MILITANCY IN KASHMIR

The Untold Saga of Counter Insurgency Operations

MILITANCY IN KASHMIR

The Untold Saga of Counter Insurgency Operations

A C SONEJA

Foreword by

Lt Gen G.L. Bakshi, PVSM (Retd)

PENTAGON PRESS

Militancy in Kashmir : The Untold Saga of Counter Insurgency Operations
A C Soneja

First Published in 2015

ISBN 978-81-8274-814-9

Published by
PENTAGON PRESS
206, Peacock Lane, Shahpur Jat,
New Delhi-110049
Phones: 011-64706243, 26491568
Telefax: 011-26490600
email: rajan@pentagonpress.in
website: www.pentagonpress.in

Branch:
Flat No.213, Athena-2,
Clover Acropolis,
Viman Nagar,
Pune-411014
Email: pentagonpresspune@gmail.com

Printed at Aegean Offset Printers, Greater Noida, U.P.

Dedicated to

All ranks of the 'BODYGUARD'

Battalion for their bravery, exemplary

Service and Sacrifice

A Tribute to a Great Soldier

L/Hav Nek Singh, KC, SC
(Posthumous) 2 JAK RIF

CONTENTS

FOREWORD

It was around 1989–90 that yet another phase of insurgency as always strongly aided and abetted by Pakistan commenced in the Valley and spread virulently and viciously all over the countryside. By the time 2 JAK RIF (BODYGUARD) was inducted into the Valley in April 1992, the insurgency was nearly at its peak, characterized by widespread killings and expulsions from the Valley, mainly of Kashmiri Pandits, all of which posed a formidable challenge to the security forces then deployed in the Valley to fight this menace. This book records the exceptional performance of the 'BODYGUARD' Battalion of the Jammu and Kashmir Rifles in the anti-insurgency operations undertaken by it in the Kashmir Valley from April 1992 to April 1995.

During the period up to 14 January 1993, when the Battalion was commanded by Col J.S. Chandel, VSM, the battalion's involvement in the operations was some what low key. This was primarily due to it being new to the game and operating under 31 Sub Area in Srinagar with numerous restrictions. The tempo of operations picked up after Col (later Lt Gen) A.C. Soneja assumed the command of the battalion on 15 January 1993 and its reversion to the parent formation. Thereafter, the performance of the battalion came into greater focus on account of the superlative results it achieved, drawing praise and commendation, repeatedly, not only from the Army hierarchy from the Brigade Commander to the Chief of the Army Staff but also equally from the civil administration in J&K, particularly the Governor. This fact is hugely indicative of the kind of impact the Battalion made by its presence and performance in whichever area of the Valley it was deployed.

The narrative is the saga of boldness and bravery, fearlessness and courage, enthusiasm and motivation, mutual trust and faith, professional competence and dynamism, and, qualitatively, exceptional kind of leadership displayed at all functional levels which, possibly, put the Battalion's performance in a somewhat different genre altogether.

This book illustrates the nuances of conducting 'Small Team Operations', which are the natural and inevitable ingredient of anti-insurgency operations of the kind carried out in the Kashmir Valley. Such operations, for their success, greatly depend upon the troops' knowledge of and adherence to 'basic tactics and their norms'. The book also highlights the necessity for the leader, especially during the planning and execution process, to innovate and make such functional/operational changes that avoid 'stereotyped and predictable' actions in terms of 'routine and timings' to be followed and with regards to choosing more difficult and hazardous terrain options in order to checkmate the insurgents so as to achieve success.

The book also highlights two other important aspects relating to such operations. First, the troops and the officers willingly and enthusiastically carry out and accomplish their tasks even when pushed against 'time', and severe privations by way of 'denial of food and rest', provided the seniors (the commanding officer, company commanders and so on) adopt consultative approach by involving their subordinates in the planning process, as also equally share and bear the hardships. Second, the importance of harnessing the goodwill and support of the civilians, especially within the area of operations and in adjacent areas, by dealing with their issues in a sympathetic manner and by adopting a humane, empathetic, transparent and fair approach has been emphasized.

I am personally aware, as I was then serving at Army Headquarters, that this very Battalion (BODYGUARD) with, by and large, the same complement of 'men and officers', but under another commanding officer, passed through a very rough patch in 1989 during 'OP PAWAN', when it did not perform well and suffered a disastrous ambush in Sri Lanka. In the Kashmir Valley, the same Battalion had created history by undertaking 581 operations, of which over 25 per cent were successfully conducted, resulting in killing/capturing of 358 insurgents and winning 86 awards as against 77 won previously in 100 years (1891–1991). This is a strong reflection on the quality of leadership that Col Soneja provided to the Battalion.

During June 1994, after visiting the Battalion as Colonel of the Regiment, I had met the then Corps Commander (who later became Chief of the Army Staff), Lt Gen S. Padmanabhan, VSM. He told me that the 'BODYGUARD' under Col Soneja was the 'BEST' battalion of his corps and he had the confidence, like his entire corps staff, that if Col Soneja or anyone in the Battalion gets a hint about the presence of any insurgent at a particular place, they 'NEED NO ORDERS, BUT WILL PURSUE THE INSURGENTS ON THEIR OWN AND EITHER APPREHEND THEM OR KILL THEM'. What high praise indeed for Col Soneja and BODYGUARD!

I sincerely believe that this book will be of great interest and value to all, particularly to the junior leaders in infantry, in understanding the nuances of conducting successful anti-insurgent operations in an environment of the kind that prevails in J&K even today.

Gurn Bakshi

Lt Gen G.L. Bakshi, PVSM (Retd),
Colonel of the Regiment Jak RIF & Ladakh Scouts
March 1990-July 1994

PREFACE

'Second Battalion', the Jammu and Kashmir Rifles also called "BODY GUARD", having been blooded in 'OP PAWAN' Sri Lanka and followed by 'OP RAKSHAK' in Punjab, drove through the Jawahar tunnel in the fading hours of 18 April 1992, for another very eventful tenure. A tenure that was extremely rewarding and satisfying. Exactly three years later as the battalion drove through the great tunnel once again, it filled everyone's heart with tremendous satisfaction. Satisfaction driving, from the feeling that they had made a small but convincing contribution in bringing peace to the troubled valley.

The Battalion commenced its move outwards on 22 April 95 from the beautiful Tral Valley, its home since January that year. The convoy was minus eight of its brave soldiers. Sub Omkar Singh Manhas and seven other brave boys had left their permanent mark in the valley. They made the supreme sacrifice in service to the 'Nation'. The martyrs included our 'bravest of the brave' Lance/Havildar Nek Singh, Kirti Chakra, Shaurya Chakra. Besides these eight, 51 other ranks including eight officers and five JCOs who were seriously injured in numerous operations, also left their permanent mark of selfless devotion and dedication with their blood.

After a two week orientation capsule in April 1992 the battalion settled down in Haft Chinar in the heart of Srinagar city under 31 Sub Area. This was its first permanent location in the valley. It moved five times again and was deployed in Prisal–Yaripura sector of Kulgam Tehsil (February–June 1993), Manasbal– Bandipur (July-December 1993), Avantipur–Panchgam (January-March 1994), Prisal–Yaripura (March-December 1994) and finally at Tral Avantipur (January-April 1995). All these areas were infested with terrorists or as we then called them Anti National Elements or militants. The battalion carried out a record 581 operations, 192 of these were successful. This resulted in recovery of 247 weapons besides a large quantity of ammunition and explosives. The hierarchy of militants neutralized included one supreme commander, Sheikh Abdul Aziz also called 'Father of Militancy in Jammu &Kashmir', three district commanders, four battalion commanders and numerous company, platoon and section commanders belonging to various tanjims.

The heroic efforts of the battalion were repeatedly applauded by number of senior commanders. A total of 44 complementary messages were received during the tenure. These included 8 from Chief of the Army Staff, 9 from General Officer Commanding-in-Chief Northern Command, 8 from General Officer Commanding 15 Corps and over two dozen from other General Officers Commanding and Brigade Commanders. The unit also received the prestigious award of 'Unit Citation' from Chief of Army Staff on 15 January 1994, a silver plaque from 'His Excellency' the Governor of J&K for outstanding performance on 13 September 1994 and finally a Unit Appreciation from GOC-in-C Northern Command on 29 March 1995. The Battalion also earned 86 awards in J&K making it the most decorated battalion of the regiment.

The list of gallantry awards included one Kirti Chakra, four Shaurya Chakras, 14 Sena Medals, one Vasisht Sewa Medal, 22 Commendation Cards from Chief of the Army Staff and 44 from GOC-in-C Northern Command.

The Battalion concluded its tenure in OP RAKSHAK (J&K) not on 22 April 1995 the day we left the Kashmir valley but four weeks later at the holy shrine of 'Mata Vaishno Devi' where it had gone to pay obeisance to DURGE MATA and thank her for her continued blessings and good wishes which made our tenure in the Valley an astounding success. It made a permanent mark in northern command and proved for itself that this battalion was indeed '**Second to None**'. It had added a golden chapter to its wonderful history of bravery and sacrifice. All ranks worked like a team always willing to live and fight together. The results were there for every one to see, 86 awards in three years was a record created with the hardwork of all ranks, the results suddenly pushed the unit to the top slot in the

'Regiment' as one of the most decorated units. A list of awards won by the unit both Pre and Post Independence are given in appendix of this book.

The aim of putting down these events on paper is to keep a record of the gallant operations under taken by all ranks of the unit during its tenure in the Jammu and Kashmir valley in a period which saw peak insurgency, breakdown of law and order, rampant killings mostly of Kashmiri Pandits and their forceful expulsions from the valley. We needed to record these events lest they be forgotten once the current combine of officers, JCO's and our brave troops say good bye to the service. It was undoubtedly a very tough period for all of us. All roads were damaged and most wooden bridges burnt. Movement on the roads, remain vulnerable to frequent ambushes, planting of improvised explosive devices and gun fire. Radio connectivity and communications both the surface as well as air, had broken down. Those who stayed close to Tropo centres were slightly better. They were occasionally able to utilize the services by giving incentive to the operators. For the majority of the troops, the beautiful land of 'heaven' had turned nearly into a hell.

In every village where we travelled, we saw numerous houses having been burnt down, their corrugated tin sheets removed, houses ransacked and every thing worthwhile removed. Such was the vitiated atmosphere. At one stage it appeared that the valley might go out of our hands. Mercifully the God Almighty was on the side of the security forces and despite numerous follies the country has stayed together.

A lot has been written on the Kashmir issue in the past sixty years. Therefore we do not intend to start over once again from Partition in August 1947 and signing of the Stand Still Agreement. We also do not intend to discuss the terrain of the beautiful valley or its geography or the role of various political leaders and the parties. This is purely a military history record of events of a brave battalion being written with an aim to provide young generations, an opportunity to learn from the experiences of their elders. A very brief description of the valley is of course included.

A C Soneja

Area of Operations of 2 JAK RIF 1992-1995

ACKNOWLEDGEMENT

I was fortunate to serve in BODYGUARD battalion twice, first time when it was deployed in High Altitude area in Arunachal Pradesh in 1985 and again from 1993 when I was posted to command this unit. I was impressed with the hardwork, sincerity and simplicity of the men in the unit. Their outstanding performance, gallantry and dedication in operations gave me the inspiration to record these events. So my first set of thanks goes to all ranks of this brave unit who worked so hard and motivated me to try and record our history of that wonderful period.

Large number of officers and men have helped me work on this book. Without their guidance and assistance it would not have been possible to complete it in this shape. My thanks to Lt Gen G L Bakshi, Lt Gen S S Grewal. Lt Gen Rameshwar Roy, Lt Gen G S Katoch, Brig V K Saxena, Col Lakhbinder and Col Gulshan Chadha for their help in collating the data, its verification and presentation. My sincere thanks to each one of them as also to Col M S Kumar and Hav Mandal who helped me in designing the book.

I also wish to thank our children Varun and Tarun who helped me from time to time in typing, setting and recovering lost data on numerous occasions. Their wives Palka and Pallavi helped me go through the drafts and thereby improve the final script; my thanks to all of them.

Finally, I wish to most earnestly thank Mr Rajan Arya, CEO Pentagon Press for undertaking this publication and for giving numerous suggestions on layout and presentation. Thanks for timely publication. You have been most accommodating. Thanks once again to you and to your complete team particularly to Mr Jeevan Nair and Mr V K Negi for their editorial assistance.

List of Maps and Sketches

DETAILS OF APPENDICES

1 Letter from Gen BC Joshi, PVSM, AVSM, ADC, (Chief of Army Staff)

2 Message from COAS-Op Hazratbal

3 Letter from Lt Gen S Padmanabhan, VSM

4 Letter from Lt Gen JS Dhillon, YSM

5 Letters from Lt Gen GL Bakshi, PVSM, ADC

6 Copy of Unit Special Part 1 Order dated 20 Apr 1995

7 Letter from Maj Gen (later Lt Gen) SS Grewal PVSM, AVSM, SM, VSM

8 Letter from Maj Gen DB Shaketkar, VSM (later Lt Gen)

9 Letter from Maj Gen RS Mavi, AVSM, SC

10 Letter from Lt Col (Retd) OP Singh, (Veteran 2 JAK RIF)

11 DO Letter from Sub (Retd) KC Photra (Veteran 2 JAK RIF)

12 Article by François Gautier, a Journalist from France

13 Tribute to L/Hav Nek Singh, KC, SC

14 Details of Armed Encounters

15 Details of Casualties

16 Detail of Gallantry Awards

17 Recovery of Warlike Stores

ABBREVIATIONS

amn	Ammunition
Bde	Brigade
Bn	Battalion
BSF	Border Security Force
CO	Commanding Officer
Comd	Command
Corps	Corps
Div	Division
dply	Deployment
gren	Grenade
Hav	Havildar
HQs	Headquarters
JCO	Junior Commissioned Officer
KC	Kirti Chakra
Mtn Bde	Mountain Brigade
Mtn Div	Mountain Division
Mtn	Mountain
NCO	Non Commissioned Officer
Nk	Naik
Offr	Officer
Op	Operation
ptl	Patrol
SC	Shaurya Chakra
SM	Sena Medal
VSM	Vashist Sewa Medal

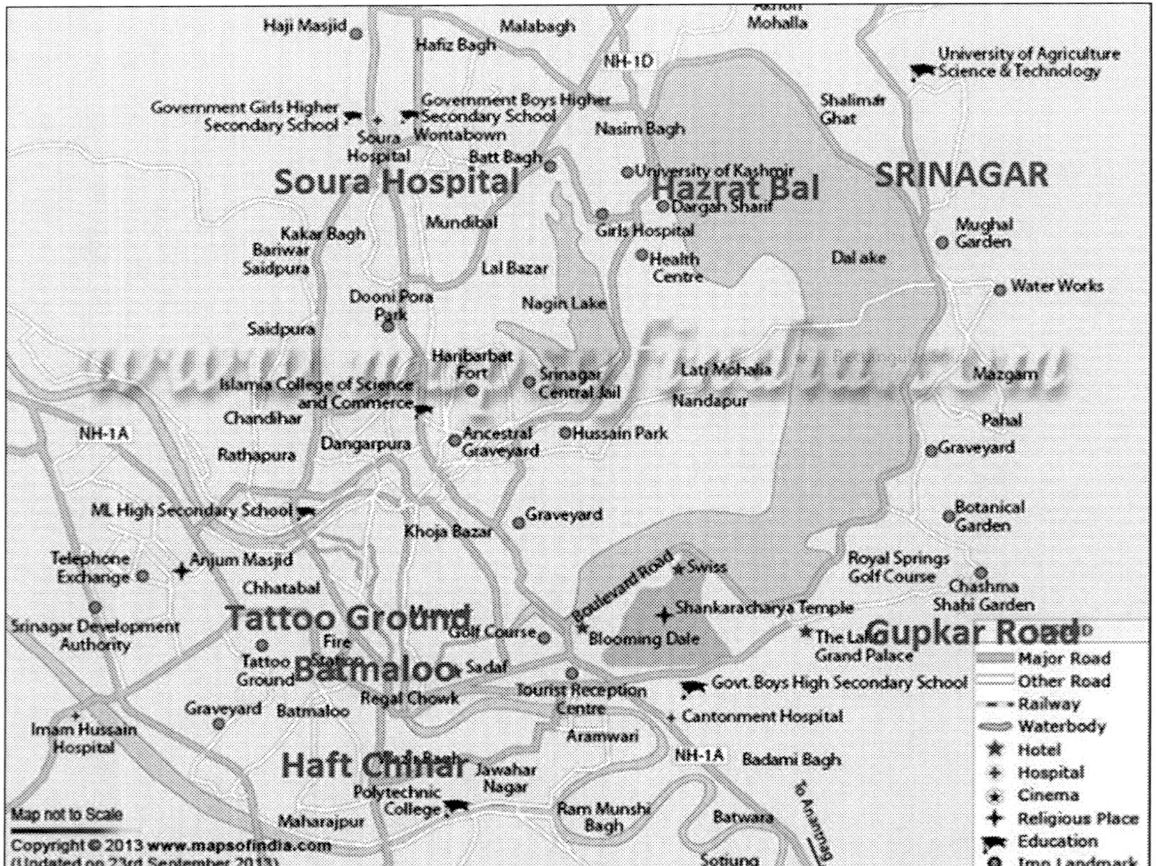

Map of Srinagar City
(Haft Chinar—Our Abode from Apr 1992 to Feb 1993)

Kashmir in Turmoil

The beautiful valley of Kashmir that was once named 'Paradise on earth' by Emperor Jahangir lies between the Great Himalayan range and the Pir Panjal ranges. It is 135 Km long and 32 Km wide. Almost in the centre of the valley floor, flows the Jhelum river that emanates from Verinag which lies close to the Northern end of Jawahar tunnel. Kashmir valley is one of the three administered divisions of the state. It consists of Anantnag, Baramula, Bandipur, Budgam, Gandharbal, Kupwara, Kulgam, Pulwama, Shopian, and Srinagar districts.

The valley floor has an average height of about 5000 feet which rises to over 15000 both in the north towards the great Himalayan range and in the south and west towards the Pir Panjal. In the east lies the Zanskar ranges. The valley has a moderate climate, while the summers are mild, winters are extremely cold. During the winters the valley experiences very heavy snowfall. The Gulmarg valley (about 8800 feet) for example experienced 14 feet of snow in 1990. In 1994 during our tenure, winters were severe, and the valley was cut off from rest of the country. We had no fresh vegetables for nearly two weeks. During this period we cherished varieties of food made from potatoes and brinjals.

Kashmir was a hindu state till the 14 century. Islam was adopted by the people in the same century under Shah Mir. His dynasty ruled up to the 16 century when it was overthrown by the Chaks. Later it was annexed by Emperor Akbar and came under the Mughal Empire. Kashmir was also ruled by the Afghans who were defeated by the Sikhs under Maharaja Ranjit

Singh in the early 19 century. Sikhs were defeated by the British in 1845 and their erstwhile empire split. The J&K state came to be ruled by the Dogra kings under an 'Agreement' signed between the Dogra rular Maharaja Gulab Singh and the British in 1846. The decedents of Maharaja Gulab Singh ruled the state till 1947 as a subordinate to the British. The last king, Maharaja Hari Singh signed the Instrument of accession on 26 October 1947 when Pakistan invaded the state.

Lord Mountbatten while accepting the document added an adjunct to it saying that the will of the people would be ascertained once the hostilities are over and the invading forces have withdrawn which never happened. In 1951 the J&K Assembly passed a resolution that the 'Accession' was final. It is also true that of the 52 members of the State Assembly most had been elected unopposed. Some people claimed that many of the members were not the true representatives of the people. Pakistan meanwhile after the 1947-48 war again tried to forcibly annex Jammu and Kahsmir in 1965, 1971 and again in 1999. They failed in each attempt. In 1965 Pakistan had trained and infilterated 30000 militants (as part of Gibralter Force), a move that was rejected by the people of the valley. In 1988-89 once again they trained and armed over 30000 militants in the valley and sent hundreds of Mujahids from Pakistan and Afghanistan.

These militants once again set up a proxy war and tried to forcibly annex the valley to Pakistan. They firstly forced the Kashmiri Pandits to flee, burnt most of the bridges and culverts, and damaged the roads so as to restrict movement of the security forces. This of course restricted their movement too. They started firing at the camps and regularly ambushed our convoys. Though initially they caused considerable damage however this move was also rejected by the people with the assistance of the security forces who managed to neutralise most of these misguided youth. It took the state machinery over 20 years and numerous sacrifices to control the situation. **It is in this role of anti militancy operations that we moved in to the beautiful valley in April 1992.**

CHAPTER 1

Operations Carried Out From 18 April 1992 to 14 January 1993

Our battalion was inducted into the Jammu and Kashmir Valley on 18 April 1992. It was initially deployed in the old airfield in Srinagar where it carried out two weeks pre-induction training under the command of Col JS Chandel, Vashist Sewa Medal, before being launched into extensive operations against terrorists in Srinagar and Pulwama districts. While the battalion was assigned to 81 Mountain Brigade located in Malang Pura, near Avantipur airfield, the battalion less two companies was also assigned to carry out operations under HQ 31 Sub Area which was then commanded by Brigadier (later Major General) JS Kanwar VSM. The battalion was deployed in Haft Chinar near Bakshi stadium which was the erstwhile location of Jammu & Kashmir Light infantry Regimental Centre.

In a series of operations conducted between May and June 1992 the battalion apprehended a number of terrorists and also recovered a large number of weapons and ammunition. On 30 May 1992 Subedar Sidhi Bahadur Mal of Alpha Company under Major Ghanshyam Katoch (now Lt Gen) managed to apprehend two terrorists after a brief fire fight. Six AK-56 rifles were recovered. The militants had hidden these in a village pond. During this operation the Junior Commission Officer (JCO) also apprehended a terrorist who had been hiding in the pond for 14hours at a stretch. He had taken cover in the bushes and only his head was above water. Three weeks later on 25 Jun 1992, Second Lieutenant (now Lieutenant Colonel) Gulshan Chadha had a chance encounter in the area of Bunagund resulting in the recovery of two AK 56 Rifles. However the militants managed to escape. Later Major HK Tiwari, Sena Medal (now Brigadier), and boys of Bravo Company apprehended a militant who was a group commander of Al-Jehad and recovered another AK 56 rifle with two magazines of ammunition from him.

Earlier on 5 Jun 1992 the battalion carried out a cordon and search operation in village Gauripura. During the identification parade eight dreaded terrorists of Mujahideen Tanjim were apprehended. There was intense reaction from the villagers particularly from the women who got together and started throwing stones at the unit personnel. Havildar Ghasita Ram of Delta Company suddenly saw a woman trying to keep low. She had been surrounded by other women. He immediately inquired and was told that the particular lady was mentally unstable. There seemed to be something abnormal about her. Havildar Ghasita Ram realized that, despite provocation of pelting of stones he could not open fire. He handed over his weapon to a comrade and approached her for a closer look.

The moment he stepped towards her she tried to run away. Showing extreme presence of mind he leapt forward and managed to hold her by her hair. To his utter surprise it came off in his hands. He immediately realized that it was a terrorist who had dressed himself as a woman. He closed in and immediately grabbed him. He turned out to be a Pakistani trained terrorist belonging to Al-Jehad. On further interrogation the terrorist handed over six AK rifles with a large number of rifle magazines and ammunition. Havildar Ghasita Ram was aptly awarded a commendation card by the Chief of Army Staff for bravery, courage and presence of mind.

On 7 July 1992 the battalion carried out a bold operation in the area of Aloochi Bagh that overlooked the premises of Haft Chinar. The terrorists had fired at our camp from the high rise buildings located on the western side of the complex. Major Avtar Singh in a swift action and with a handful of men immediately reacted. He jumped over the boundary wall and chased the terrorists. After a quick fire fight the terrorists withdrew leaving behind two AK-56 rifles which were duly recovered. Maj Avtar Singh, was awarded a Sena Medal in January 1993. The unit also participated in a successful operation conducted by 56 and 81 Mountain Brigades in Kralpura, Srinagar.

The success in the operation was commended by the Army Commander who sent us first of his numerous messages.

The unit also carried out an operation in Batmaloo on 29 November. During the search of the area, a terrorist hiding inside a house was apprehended. He turned out to be a battalion commander of Al Jehad. Major Harsh Tiwari worked on him and was able to motivate him to hand over his weapon and we recovered an AK 47 Rifle with a magazine and 30 rounds of ammunition.

For the next month and a half we continued to stay in Haft Chinar and carried out extensive training particularly in toning up of minor tactics and battle drills. During this period we were occasionally tasked by 31 Sub Area and sometimes by Headquarters 81 Mountain Brigade for cordon and search operations. Operationally the period was not fruitful since they did not yield positive results. Some of the young officers like Major (now Colonel) R S K Nair were forced to undertake academic classes in preparation for their promotion examinations, much against their wishes. They however, subsequently acknowledged that the effort was extremely beneficial.

The last day of the year 1992 brought us the much awaited No 3 Selection Board results for 1972 batch. Lieutenant Colonel A C Soneja the second in command was approved for promotion to the rank of colonel. A week later came his posting order to take over command by 15 January 1993. Col J S Chandel, VSM was posted to 87 Mountain Brigade as the Deputy Brigade Commander. This formation was located in Himachal Pradesh but came back to our area of operations in less than four months.

CHAPTER 2

Details of Operations Conducted From 15 January 1993

January 1993 saw a change of command in the battalion on Army Day. Col J S Chandel, VSM who had very successfully commanded the battalion since April 1989 proceeded on posting and Lt Col A C Soneja took over as 42nd commanding officer of the unit. The State celebrations for the Republic day were scheduled in Bakshi Stadium in Srinagar. The areas that could interfere in the celebrations were selected for carrying out sanitization. Batmaloo was our target for the 25th. We opened our account for the year by apprehending one terrorist and recovered from him one AK-47 rifle with one magazine and 30 rounds. The apprehension was very interesting. Batmaloo was a hotbed of militancy. It had a very large number of terrorists and an equal number of policemen, all located around the Police Control Room [PCR] near the J&K Assembly building.

On that day we had collected all the able bodied men in the respective company areas of responsibility for better management and control. In rural areas and villages we normally used to assemble all able bodied men at one convenient place. Since Batmaloo was a densely populated area, we did that company wise, otherwise it would have been difficult to control and manage. While going through Alpha Company commanded by Major Ghanshyam Katoch we saw a young and a simple looking boy of about 18 years trying to hide his face. He was immediately called out. The

Commanding Officer (CO) spoke to him for about half an hour, all the time insisting that he was a terrorist. Though he initially denied being one, he suddenly agreed that he had a weapon tucked away in a garage in Lal Chowk. This was another dreaded area which was not under cordon that day. We quickly gathered an adhoc Quick Reaction Team (QRT) since the CO QRT with Harbans had gone to Headquarters 15 Corps intelligence branch for picking up an apprehended terrorist to help us in identification of suspects in Batmaloo. We did not want to waste time and wait for the CO QRT. It was decided to react immediately and we gathered the CO jeep, a one ton vehicle and an ambulance that were readily available. The Commanding Officer and Adjutant Captain (now Colonel) Lakhbinder (fondly called Lakhi) with a handful of boys took the young boy who had just admitted of being a terrorist, to a market in Lal Chowk area. Fortunately the markets were closed due to a bandh call given by anti-national elements in view of the impending Republic day celebrations.

This bandh call was actually a help to us. All streets were deserted. In a few minutes the particular garage was located. Thereafter the boy told us that he did not have the key to the lock of the garage. Our man of all seasons Havildar Nek Singh was there to resolve the issue. He took out a bunch of keys from his pocket and tried some of them. Fortunately he managed to open the lock and we found an AK rifle that had elluded us for almost two months.

Next day we were deployed in Patushai Bagh and in Bemina area before noon and in Jama Masjid Area in 'downtown' Srinagar in the afternoon. There was a brief encounter in the morning in Patushahi Bagh in which we recovered one magazine with 29 rounds of AK rifle. There was a terrorist who when challenged opened fire, and ran away. We were not alert and failed to catch him as the thick foliage and darkness helped him to escape. We learnt our lesson and ensured that such mistakes were not repeated.

On 27 January we reverted to Headquarters 81 Mountain Brigade and the next day decided to carry out a reconnaissance in force in our new area of responsibility which lay between Srinagar and Pulwama. The route that we selected was to take us to Tsar-re-Sharif and Pakharpur and then down to Pulwama, and via Pampore back to Srinagar. We decided to take the CO QRT and one rifle company only and return to Haft Chinar in Srinagar by 6 PM the same day and prepare for yet another operation that was already planned for the next day. On 29 January we were to carry out a cordon and search operation of the politically sensitive town of Biz Bihara as part of a two 'brigade operation'. 11 RAJ RIF and 2 JAK RIF of 81 Mountain Brigade and 1 Rashtriya Rifles (RR) battalion of I Sector RR. The operation was to be controlled by headquarters 1 Sector RR.

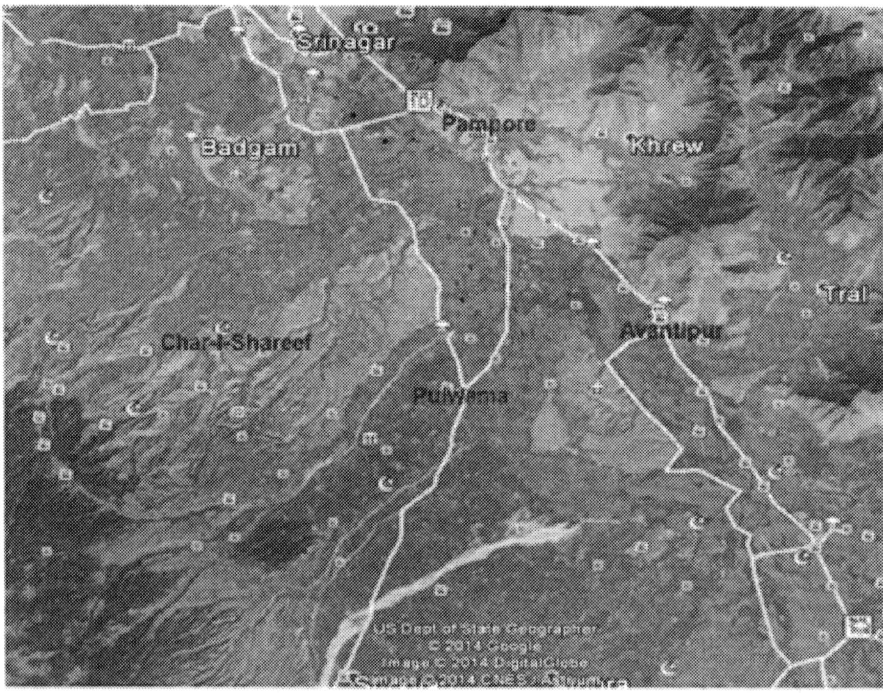

Area of Ops-Srinagar-Char-i-Shareef-Pulwama-Srinagar, 28 Jan 1993

Our reconnaissance in force on 28 January was once again very interesting. We picked up a few suspected individuals but released them soon, after a quick on the spot interrogation. Later we enjoyed our packed lunch in the salubrious surroundings of the beautiful valley. In the evening we crossed the Romushi river and were smoothly heading towards Kakapur and on to Srinagar to be back well in time for dinner and to prepare for the next day's operation in Biz Bihara. All around in the countryside the entire area was completely white with snow. Throughout the day we had tried our best to keep away from tracks covered by snow. In the evening while passing through one of the villages one of our three ton vehicles got stuck in the snow. We tried to push it manually but failed. Tractors were requisitioned, initially one and later two. Even with two tractors the vehicle just refused to budge.

Delay of minutes changed to hours and from 5 PM it soon became 10 PM. All the boys were without food since we were not carrying dinner and were expecting to reach Half Chinar well before dinner time. Harbans the battalion second in command suggested we buy biscuits. That was a good idea and we bought a packet each for everyone. That was a 20th century dinner for the troops. We repeated this on a number of occasions during our tenure in the valley. Villages and shops were in plenty and eatables were no problem. With operations uppermost in our mind the food was never a limiting factor thereafter.

While we were stuck everyone up the line was getting worried. Worried about us and for the next day's important operation. Subedar Major Roshan Lal Pathania our unit SM was anxiously waiting in Half Chinar. At about 10.30 PM Harbans volunteered to go to our brigade headquarters at Malangpura to get a recovery vehicle. He returned two hours later followed by a company of 22 Grenadiers which relieved us at 1 AM. And an hour later instead of going to Half Chinar in Srinagar, we went to 11 RAJ RIF at Malangpura. After a two hour rest, and a quick wash we were off again alongwith 11 RAJ RIF, to Biz Bihara which we cordoned off by 5 AM. Three hours later we commenced the search of the town. Despite six hours of search there was no outcome and no recoveries or apprehensions. The town had witnessed firing on our GOC's convoy only three days earlier, which indicated the presence of terrorists but we failed to catch them.

In the afternoon we had a conference of two Brigade Commanders and the three Commanding officers in the area of the famous Mughal Gardens. It was brought out by Commander 1 Sector RR and their CO that the militants generally fired from across the Jhelum River which flows from east to west almost parallel to the national highway with the Mughul Gardens in between. The CO I RR also revealed that the militants usually kept sentries across the river on the only bridge in the town, both by day and night. He recommended that we launch a two company operation at night to search and destroy these sentries. Brig A S Khanna, Vir Chakra, our commander, asked the Sector Commander 1 RR as to who would command the operation. The Sector Commander said he would do that himself since the area fell within his area of responsibility. Next, our

Commander asked him, where exactly would he be, "in my operations room at Khanabal," he immediately retorted. Though every headquarter had an operations room, our bedrooms those days were also as good as operation rooms. It appeared that Commander 1 Sector RR would command the operation from his room itself. Sensing trouble CO "BODYGUARD" volunteered to lead the operation and to personally take approval from Commander 1 Sector RR before leaving the area. This was immediately agreed to by both commanders. Around 1600 h while Commander 81 Infantry Brigade and 11 RAJ RIF left for Malangpura, 2 JAK RIF along with 1 RR Battalion came to Khanabal.

A brief halt of about three hours and we were back on our feet. In order to maintain surprise we walked down to Bij Bihara a distance of 5 km along the National Highway from Khanabal. There was no movement, neither of any vehicle nor of any human being or any animal. We were confident that we would get some success that night and the time would not be wasted. A two pronged access to the bridge was made, which we crossed but found nothing. After a brief search of the area we called off the operation by about 2330 h that day and after taking due permission from Commander 1 Sector RR we called for our vehicles from Khanabal and returned to Half Chinar well past midnight, all safe and sound but with no results.

On 1 February 93 our Commander visited us in Half Chinar. Before leaving, he directed us to plan an operation for cordon and search of village Midura in Tral tehsil of Pulwama district. A large number of militants were reported to be staying there. Later in the evening he informed us that a small village which was just north of Midura was the target and not Midura that he had told us earlier. None had seen the village so the plan for approach to the village was made from the map. Midura lies along the western slopes of the Tral valley which is part of Avantipur tehsil of Pulwama district. Our Brigade Headquarters was located in Malangpura due west of Avantipur and the Jhelum River. Though 11 RAJ RIF was co-located with Headquarters the Commander decided to give this task to us, primarily to surprise the terrorists.

The villages of Midura and Nanar are shown in the map on the following page. The map also show location of Avantipur town which is

30 Km from Srinagar, with reference to the target villages and the Brigade Headquarters.

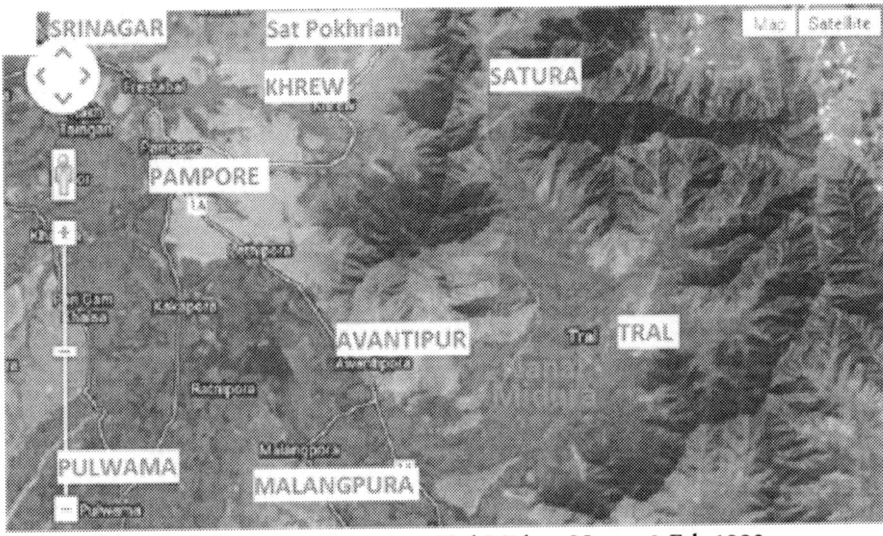

Area of Operations Avantipur-Tral-Midura-Nanar, 2 Feb 1993

Movement out of Srinagar was difficult to hide, particularly at night since no one ventured out due to the fear of militant or retaliatory fire from the security forces. Any movement out of Half Chinar was also seen by sentries at the two police stations located just outside. We decided to change our plans for movement to the concerned area and therefore requisitioned a matador and a truck to lead our way so as to achieve surprise. Led by the CO QRT, Harbans in the truck and Captain Paramjot Singh Virk in the matador followed by rest of the battalion in service transport we left Srinagar at 0200 h on 2 February 1993.

The road to Midura takes off from Avantipur. So, short of Avantipur, we increased our gap with the civil transport. While the civil truck and the matador turned towards Midura, the CO QRT continued for five Km on the national highway, it was appreciated that the militants might have some look out sentries on hill tops astride the Tral valley, and if they were there, they would appreciate that this particular column had moved towards east in the direction of Biz Bihara and Anantnag and was not headed towards the Tral valley. It later transpired that there was no system of deploying sentries by the militants. The remaining battalion stopped short of Avantipur. After travelling for five Km the CO QRT turned back and returned to Avantipur and then turned towards Midura followed by the remaining battalion.

Enroute to Midura we found that the matador had unfortunately got stuck, Paramjot was instructed to get down and quickly move to the objective, walk or run whatever he preferred, but he was ordered to reach in time. It was almost 5 AM by then. The dawn had not broken. We tried to complete the cordon, however, the two companies took time to close up. To the west of the village there is a ridge line which we covered very well. Towards the east there is broken ground. Since we were not familiar with the layout of the village, the flank towards the east was not covered well till the companies closed in which took nearly another hour. To our horror and disgust we learnt that a large group had managed to escape through. Suddenly we saw some suspicious movement about a km away to the east. The complete CO QRT and Alpha company commander Major Ghanshyam Katoch immediately took off and chased the suspected terrorists for nearly two Km. We got nothing and returned to Nanar where by then all the men folk had been collected near the primary school.

Around 8 AM we started our search of the village. Three search parties from each company accompanied by some village elders and a few volunteers, started a systematic house to house search very well knowing that our target had managed to escape. Nevertheless all ranks were motivated to put in their best and to find if there was anyone hiding in the village. Two hours later while searching through a store shed used for fodder, a patrol led by Company Havildar Major Satpal Singh of Charlie company was all of a sudden challenged by a short burst through the haystack. The bullets hit one of the civilian boys who was accompanying the patrol. Satpal immediately retaliated hitting the militant and dropping him dead before he could do any more harm. This was the first physical elimination of the year, that was repeated numerous times in the months ahead.

We later learnt that there was a group of about 10 to 15 militants staying in the village that night. All of them except their leader managed to get away. He stayed back since he was not well and hence the encounter. This was the first major success of the battalion but we did not rejoice, because we knew we had actually failed. After the operation we sat down together and discussed our weaknesses and failures. A number of lessons were learnt. We were determined to learn and overcome our weaknesses and to ensure that such mistakes were not repeated. Every one was advised to take quick decisions whenever they were stuck in a similar situation. As long as the main aim of curbing militancy was kept in mind all actions undertaken by junior leaders would be acceptable provided their actions were within the confines of law and instructions issued by the Chief of Army Staff.

We left Tral valley at 1500 h that day. The beautiful valley with its beautiful inhabitants called us back time and again in the next two years, and every time we came, we had deadly encounters. A number of militants were neutralised and their weapons recovered. More of it later. A few days later the General Officer Commanding 8 Mountain Division Major General R S Mavi, Shaurya Chakra, Sena Medal, paid us an unscheduled visit in Haft Chinar. He spent more than an hour in the COs' office and asked a lot of questions on gathering of intelligence, training and operations. After an hour long discussion he suddenly looked up at the photographs of ex commanding officers, and asked the CO, the name of the Commanding Officer who had encouraged all officers to take to hard drinks. This was a tricky situation since the concerned CO was in service commanding a brigade. But it wasn't possible to tell a lie either, therefore the CO had to name one of his predecessors who had this dubious distinction. The General Officer Commanding was assured that the issue of liquor to troops, hereafter would be fully controlled and the present CO who was a tea totaller, in any case, would never take to drinks at all in the valley. This assurance was by and large kept except on occasions, to celebrate outstanding events or successes like the visit of Chief of Army Staff or apprehension of Sheikh Abdul Aziz, the supreme commander of Al-Jihad who was also called the 'Father of Militancy' or award of Unit Citation by the COAS. On these occasions we did open up a bottle of champagne. That we felt was OK. The ex CO whose name came up in discussion that day suddenly got posted to the Divisional Headquarters within a month as Deputy General Officer Commanding, so the issue was closed.

The rest of the month that year saw us conducting a number of operations west of Pulwama town and around the villages of Zainapura and Chittargram of Shupian tehsil. There were number of successes too. Four days after Naner, while operating in village Nohama, Major RSK Nair scooped out a terrorist hiding inside a haystack. Two weeks later he apprehended yet another terrorist in village Chittargram. We recovered a Chinese pistol each from both these terrorists.

On 6 February after returning from a successful operation in village Nohama we were faced with a different kind of problem. There were frantic calls being made from various headquarters looking for the Commanding officer, all simultaneously crying for his head. We had just entered the campus when an operator came running to announce that there was an urgent call from the Brigadier General Staff in headquarters 15 Corps. He told the commanding officer that a lady in Aloochibagh staying about a km from the unit had alleged that, two of our boys had gone to her house and molested her, the night before. She claimed that these were the same boys who had stood outside her house on 26 January when the unit had operated in that area. There were other urgent calls too. Queries were made by the staff at Corps, Sub Area, the Division and the Brigade headquarters. The lady had gone to the PCR and to the Governor's office to lodge a complaint against us. She had apparently caused a lot of damage already.

The CO went to the police station. By chance he took Major Paramjot Virk, who had operated near her house on that particular day. In front of the DSP the lady could not identify Paramjot who despite the fact that he was the only turbanned officer in the company which had conducted the cordon and search operation near her house on 26 January. There was an open patch of ground next to her house where the men folk of the area had been collected. The CO and Paramjot even had lunch on that day while sitting near her house. Fortunately for us the lady did not recognize either the CO or the company commander. Her house lay on a route which the terrorists had been frequenting for their move towards Aloochibagh and thereafter to Batmaloo. There were numerous posters outside her house put up by the militants.

Next day in the presence of our commander Brigadier AS Khanna, Vir Chakra, the Superintendent Police Srinagar [south] interrogated the lady. This time she changed her statement and told the police officers that the boys who had come at night had their faces fully covered and she was unable to identify them. Since she could not identify the CO or the company commander there was no question of her identifying boys with their heads covered. The lady had complained that the boys were wearing white snow shoes. This she said she had seen despite the fact that it was dark. These shoes were available in plenty in the local market and could have been used by anyone. She had obviously complained under pressure from the terrorists and was unable to justify her allegations in front of senior police officers. The allegation was mercifully dropped and we were permitted to concentrate on our job at hand.

On 6 February we had apprehended one terrorist from village Nohama. He was a tough looking guy with an excellent physique. There was a strong representation from the village in his favour. His wife also pleaded for his release. Since he had a weapon, and was a confirmed Pakistan trained terrorist he had to be handed over to the police. We therefore brought him to the unit in Haft Chinar. After two days when the Aloochjbagh incident got over we received a call from a lady claiming to be his wife stating that she wanted to come and see him. The lady was allowed to meet him in the office of the CO in the presence of the second in command and the head clerk. This lady, we soon discovered, was not the one we met in the village. She was from Srinagar, obviously his second wife, was good looking and educated. Harbans casually asked the militant that most of us could not look after even one and how could he look after two? The terrorist told us that he had one to look after his responsibilities in the village and another in Srinagar city. We helped the lady take care of her immediate needs and handed over the boy to the police. We had no right to meddle in personal affairs and therefore decided to keep away.

On 12 February we went to Tral again. This time the target was Satura, a village deep inside the Tral valley. We were tasked to move to Khrew in Pampore which is about 12 Km from Srinagar by day and later at night cross the Satura ridge near Satpokhrian. The map given on page 9 shows the relative location of our halting place that is Khrew base which was the permanent location of our Divisional Artillery Brigade then. We were tasked to establish stops around Satura by 5AM and at the same time 11 RAJ RIF was to drive straight in to the valley and cordon villages of Pastun-Wagad and Lam. We started from Half Chinar at about 1100 h that day after having changed our tactical numbers on the vehicles to the one used by the Artillery Brigade. All officers temporarily changed their eppaulets from JAK RIF to Artillery. We drove to the Regulating Centre in Srinagar convoy ground and joined the Khrew convoy. We entered Khrew absolutely undetected. Rested for a couple of hours and after last light walked about five km to Satpokhrian first and then climbed the western ridge overlooking the Tral Valley.

We reached Satura early morning. The night was terribly cold, but every one controlled themselves as ordered and did not light up fires till well past first light. The CO QRT quickly went inside the village and knocked at one of the houses and woke up an old man. He was requested to take us to the house of a terrorist called Ashraf who was known to be a platoon commander of the area. He readily agreed to take us there. On arrival we quickly forced ourselves inside the house. The only male inside was another old man, the father of the terrorist. He told us that his son had not been seen for many months, and he was not aware of his whereabouts at all. A quick search of the house revealed nothing and we came back outside the village to wait for sunshine so that we could start a systematic search of the village.

Meanwhile, Major M Jogdand (Jogi) had also entered the village, he found a man walking in a suspicious manner. Jogi asked the location of the house of the same terrorist that the CO QRT was looking for. That man guided the troops to Ashraf's house, introduced them to the family and then very cleverly slipped away. That man was himself Ashraf. We realized our mistake many hours later, but by then it was too late. He just disappeared and we failed to locate him during the 24 hours that we were in the village.

At about 7.30 AM the stops of 11 RAJ RIF saw some men moving in a suspicious manner and fired at them. The men dropped a pistol and ran away. Our boys of Alpha Company also saw some movement in a nala north west of Satura village. There was a group of people there too, and they were immediately engaged by fire. Fortunately for us we failed to hit anyone. On investigation we found that there was a group of 15 Gujjars grazing their cattle. We nearly got ourselves involved in cold blooded murder. But the GOD ALMIGHTY was certainly on our side and nothing could go wrong despite our follies.

Next we saw a group of 15 to 20 young boys sitting two Km away above the village of Naristan (changed recently to Nargistan). A brief movement towards Naristan alerted them and they started running. Despite the distance and the difficulty of running uphill we chased them for two km. We even fired at them from long range, but probably did not hit them. Though they managed to escape successfully to the higher reaches, we felt that psychologically we had given them a beating. They could not thereafter boast to the local population that they had put up a fight against the Army, a boast which they often made. Later during the search of the area we found a revolver and therefore did not return empty handed. The General officer commanding 8 Mountain Division Major General R S Mavi SC, SM visited us at Naristan and complemented the unit for the operation even though the results were not very encouraging. He also told the Brigade Commander to tell the CO 2 JAK RIF to take some rest. This the Commander conveyed during a conference that he held in the evening in the outskirts of Satura. Notwithstanding that, we continued to complete our task conscientiously.

A Temple in ruins in Naristan (now called Nargistan)

We returned to Half Chinar on 13 February to continue the unfinished tasks that lay ahead. The stay in Half Chinar was very comfortable. All ranks had proper barracks to stay. Being close to the transit camp entry and exit from the valley was very convenient. The Sub Area Headquarters had already decided to push us out of the beautiful city and 6 Maratha Light Infantry of 56 Mountain Brigade was tasked to replace us. This decision was obviously taken due to our not so good performance in comparison to 10 Garhwal and 6 Maratha Light Infantry. We, all along had felt that we were not being provided with all the information and opportunity that the others were being given, nevertheless we had no one else to blame than ourselves for our poor performance. This must have prompted the Sub Area Headquarters to take that decision of moving us out of the town.

Reverting to our shifting out of Srinagar, the boys put up a number of representations to the CO against the intended change. A few of them came through the buddy of the CO. Some of the boys felt that the Commanding Officer was personally instrumental in moving out the unit from the barracks in Haft Chinar. He had to explain the reasons of the intended move to the troops in a Sainik Sammelan on 28 February. He tried to convince them that the unit had come to the valley for a specific task. In Army we are expected to move wherever and whenever ordered without any inhibition. Troops were reminded of the oath taken by every one when we joined the service. One of the lines in the oath said, "**We will go wherever ordered willingly and cheerfully**". He also told them that probably the God ALMIGHTY had better things in store for us in the days ahead as it actually proved. 86 awards and 358 terrorists neutralized by the end of the tenure would be an achievement many units would find it difficult to match.

Based on our performance in the next few months 31 Sub Area repeatedly called us back for important operations like the quelling of a strike by the J&K Police in April 1993, providing security to Amarnath Yatra in August 1993 and finally for the month long Hazratbal crises in October of the same year. To top it all, the Sub Area commander nominated CO 2 JAK RIF to provide him personal security at the end of the Hazaratbal operation in mid November 1993 when he had to return to Gupkar road. He did not take security cover from 10 Garhwal Rifles which was orbatted to 31 Sub Area and was his Regimental battalion located in Badami Bagh cantonment. Despite the fact that we had to go to Safapura area which was in the opposite direction, he asked us to provide him the security cover. That was the state of confidence that the Sub Area Commander had for the battalion in later months. The 31 Sub Area Commander repeatedly communicated with the unit to congratulate us for the next two years even after moving out on promotion to Secunderabad. However in January-February 1993 the situation was totally different. We were actually shunted out of the city.

We moved out of Half Chinar at an auspicious hour of 0200 h on 3 March to carry out a cordon and search operation in Prisal also referred to as Frisal in some maps, this was to be our abode for the next four months. Our Commander, Brig A S Khanna, VrC visited us at Prisal, at 0900 h the same day. We had barely commenced our pitching of tents and just settled down for a well deserved cup of tea when we got a message that one of our boys Rifleman (barber) Jai Singh, who was to join us in the second trip from Half Chinar had accidentally shot himself with his Self Loading Rifle (SLR). He had succumbed to his injuries before reaching the hospital. The CO QRT returned to Half Chinar for investigation while Harbans, the second in command continued to settle the unit in Prisal.

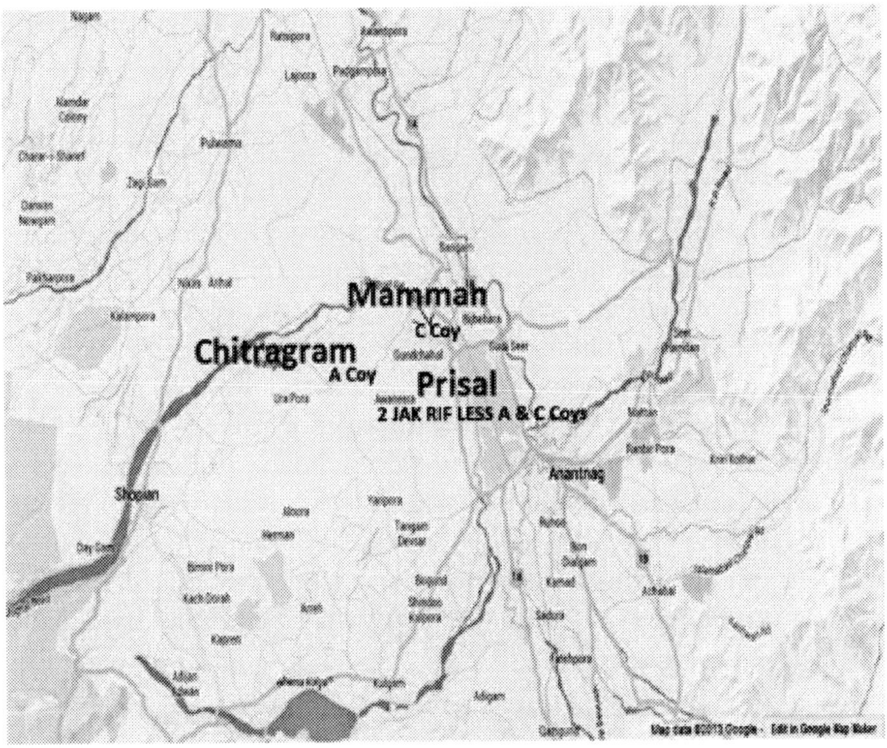

Our Deployment Areas in South Kashmir March 1993

In Prisal the Battalion Headquarters less two companies was located in the compound of the Government School which had been completely burnt down by the militants a few years earlier. The open patch overlooked the entire village and provided us good visibility of the area. The compound was beautiful with 62 high quality walnut trees and lush green fields all around. We were neighbours with two schools, one was Hanfia School and another run by the hard core, Jamait-e-Islami, an organization that supported the Hizbul Muzahideen [HM], the most notorious militant outfit in the valley. The Hanfia school in the next few months came to be called Army Public School Prisal by the terrorists since we adopted the school for certain improvements.

Of the other two companies Alpha Company under Major Ghanshyam Katoch was located at Chitargram in the barracks of the State Electricity Board and Charlie Company under Major Rajesh Sood was located in village Mamman which overlooked the area of Arwani to the north. Both these companies provided security to our convoys moving from Brigade Headquarters to our unit headquarters at Prisal. While Battalion less Alpha and Charlie companies guarded the road axis from Arwani-Prisal-Yaripura-Kulgam, Alpha and Charlie companies dominated the other road axis from Arwini-Zainapura-Chitargram-Shupian also called Shopian.

The CO QRT returned to Prisal the next day. On 5 March we carried out reconnaissance of our area on foot. Reconnaissance on foot is generally safer from the point of view of interference by the terrorists particularly when moving tactically from more than one direction. We saw the beautiful surroundings and the various tracks leading to and from our three camps. We also met some of the village heads called macdooms and generally gathered some details of the terrorists even though most people told us that all militants had disappeared as soon as we had come in to the area which we soon realized was a wrong and misleading statement. The militants were very much there, that too in large numbers and staying all around us. We therefore had to keep our wits together and try and beat them at their own game.

During our patrol through village Reban near Chitargram we found a husband wife couple spraying their apple orchard. While the man was spraying the plants his wife carried a set of two cylinders on her back. He was casually admonished for giving a difficult task to his wife. He told the CO that it was OK to give extra work to the women as they were meant for that. He was advised to be a little more humane. This man was a hardcore Jamaiti himself. He spent a few days with us later and we unsuccessfully tried to change his opinion about the Government and women. From his conversation on that day it was decided that we would re-visit the village very soon.

March 6 was the day decided for the last rites of late Rifleman Jai Singh which were carried out near the old airfield in Srinagar. Late in the evening we returned to Prisal ready to launch ourselves into our first operation after our shift to the wilderness. Reban was selected to be our first target village, located close to Chitargram where the militants had killed a number of rich Pandits in 1990-91. We were certain to find some militants there. This impression we had gathered during our conversation with villagers two days earlier. In the past few days we had observed that whenever we approached a village invariably some terrorist would fire a few shots from his rifle and warn everyone about the presence of the army. Harbans suggested that we follow the same tactics which was readily agreed to. We had also observed that in view of the 'EID' which was a few days away the men in particular were seen to be getting up very early in the morning. During this period, by about 4 AM all the men would get together in the village mosques to offer their morning prayers. It was therefore decided to cordon the village by 4 AM so that we could collect the men immediately after the morning prayers.

We left Prisal at 0200 h on 7 March and surrounded Reban the target village, by 0400 h as planned. On arrival in the village the CO QRT was split into two. Harbans with 10 boys went straight to the center of the village close to the main mosque, and fired one round in the air from his AK rifle, a weapon that was also being used by the terrorists. Meanwhile the CO QRT started moving inside the village slowly and stealthily to see if there was any movement. We had also come to the conclusion that most terrorists used to move into their hideouts after the arrival of the troops in their respective villages.

To deny them this advantage we started moving slowly and deliberately into the narrow and dark lanes and by lanes of the village. The patrol was led by our brave Havildar Nek Singh and Shamsher Singh of Intelligence and Surveillance platoon. After about 20 minutes or so, we confronted a well built man who accidentally crossed our way. He was quickly grabbed by our alert boys. The man claimed to be absolutely innocent but a careful look at him revealed that he was definitely lying. He was sporting a big beard, wearing a good quality black tracksuit and blue sports shoes. He had not gone to the village mosque for prayers like the rest of the village. There was therefore no doubt in our mind about his identity, he certainly was a terrorist.

He was handed over to Lt Col Santosh our officiating RMO who was asked to take the young man out of the village so that he could not create a hue and cry. It was apprehended that had he made some noise in the village it would have got the women of the village out and could have created some chaos and confusion. They could have even forced us to release him. The RMO was asked to psychologically work on him and to see if we could succeed. The efficient doctor that he was, Santosh worked quickly on him, who not only accepted that he indeed was a terrorist but also agreed to hand over two AK rifles to us. There was however a hitch, the weapons were tucked away in Zaina pura which was three Km away.

Harbans was immediately summoned and tasked to take the militant to Zainapura for the recovery. By about 6 AM just before daylight, we were able to inform the brigade headquarters that we had indeed recovered two AK rifles and six magazines with 180 rounds of live ammunition. We also learnt that this was the authorization of each militant given to them by their handlers across the border. This was a good start. Our spirits were high, we had made a mark on the terrorists and conveyed a clear message to them that we had arrived to carry out the serious business of bringing peace in the area and to restore law and order and Government control.

The following day was a holiday on account of Holi. The Commander invited the CO to the Brigade Headquarters at Malangpura to confer the acting rank of Colonel on him. The promotion orders had come a day earlier. After a short ceremony the CO went to Srinagar to get clearance from the police for the accidental death of late Rifleman Jai Singh. This was successfully obtained. The Commanding Officer returned to Prisal alongwith Ghanshyam and Lakhbinder who had both returned from short leave. They were happy to see that the unit was beginning to settle down quite well.

In the evening the commander visited us at Prisal where he stayed for the night in preparation for the next day's operation. This was to be a two battalion operation. The objectives were village 'Khudweni' for 1 Rashtriya Rifle Battalion from Khanabal and village 'Kaimuuh' for BODYGUARD

Battalion. These two villages lie astride Vishwa river which is a tributary of Jhelum river. These villages are about three to four kms from Khanabal-Anantnag.

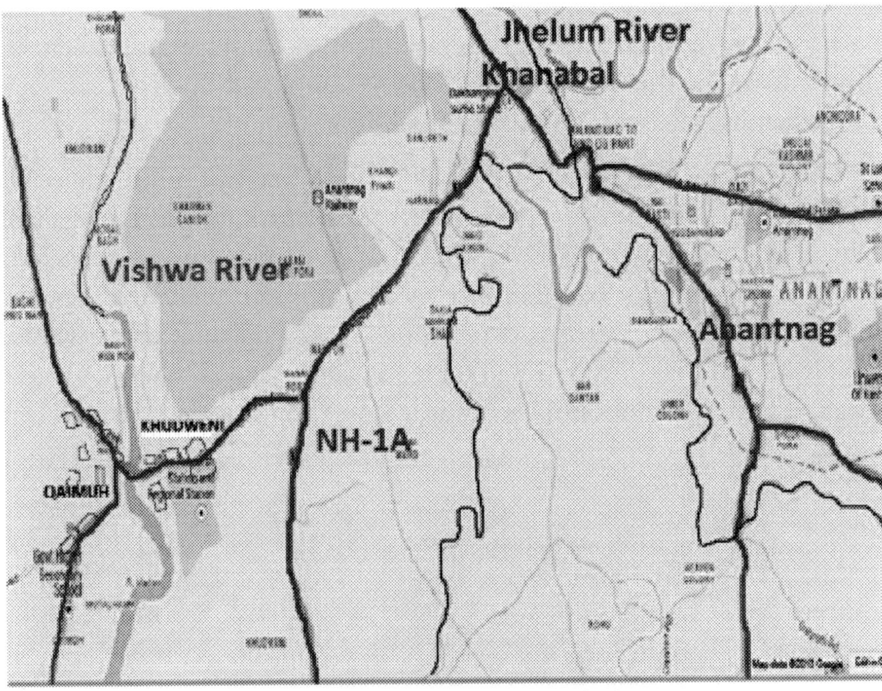

Area of Operations of Qaimuh-Khudwani

Once again we started at 2AM on 9 March and successfully cordoned the village by 0400 h. This operation was successful too. Both units made recoveries. While 1 Rashtriya Rifles recovered one AK rifle, we recovered one rocket launcher. This was our first big catch, three weapons in as many days, God Almighty and 'Durge Mata' were kind and there were no casualties to troops and no serious damage to militants too.

From 10 March till 24 April Harbans officiated as CO. During this period he consolidated the battalion's hold over the area. The terrorists were constantly on the run. A total of 11 terrorists were apprehended and three killed in various encounters. The battalion also recovered 13 weapons which included 10 AK rifles, two Universal Machine Guns (UMG) and one Rocket propelled grenade launcher (RPG). On 4 April Harbans had carried out an excellent operation near Damal Hanjipura, which lies to the south of the Vishwa river near Kulgam. In a gallant action Harbans led the boys through the icy cold waters of the river. The water was chest high but the determined troops, notwithstanding even their short height, waded through. Efforts paid good dividends indeed. A total of four terrorists were apprehended, one killed and five AK rifles recovered. As a consequence the battalion received the first Complimentary message from General Officer Commanding in Chief Northern Command in that year, who complemented all ranks for the splendid effort.

On 25 April we celebrated the 125th Raising Day of our battalion in a modest and sumptuous manner. We paid homage to all those gallant soldiers who laid down their lives while participating in various operations with the unit. Twenty two families whose wards had made the supreme sacrifice in Sri Lanka were presented with a sewing machine each. We also complemented Major Avtar Singh for his Sena Medal and other JCO's and Jawans (soldiers) who had been awarded on the occasion of Army Day and Republic Day 1993.

Recoveries – April 1993

On 27 April we apprehended yet another terrorist and recovered a pistol from him. The next day we were called up in Srinagar by HQs 31 Sub Area to assist 56 Mountain Brigade in quelling the police revolt. This was in response to the death of a police head constable in exchange of fire between militants and security forces near the holy shrine of Hazratbal.

The local police in Srinagar had locked themselves in the Police Control Room (PCR) in Batmaloo and taken a number of senior police officers as hostages. We were located at Haft Chinar as reserve for the operation. 56 Mountain Brigade managed to overpower the police personnel without much of resistance. 6 MLI of the Brigade used armoured personnel carriers to break the boundary wall and entered the fortress like PCR from an unexpected direction. Better sense prevailed. The troops and the police personnel did not fire at each other. The police personnel released all their senior officers. The operation had a peaceful ending like in the movies and we returned to Prisal on 29 April 1993.

The month of May 1993 was a violent one. We had some excellent operations during the month in which 21 terrorists were neutralised. A total of 15 AK rifles and three pistols were recovered. Harbans, Lakhbinder, Hardeep and Ashish Maini in particular spearheaded our attacks on the anti national elements. An outstanding display of gallantry and bravery by these officers resulted in historic operations which were commended by Chief of Army Staff and by General Officer Commanding in Chief Northern Command. These operations are separately discussed in detail. One operation was a lightning raid launched by a small party, 45 km from our base on 5 May and the next one was on 9 followed by another on 12 and the last on 21 May. In the last operation we had laid siege to village Nilura from where we apprehended **Sheikh Abdul Aziz, Supreme commander of El Jehad who was called Father of Militancy in J&K**. He was apprehended along with 10 of his bodyguards. We also recovered five AK rifles and three pistols.

On 2 and 9 May while the battalion carried out routine cordon and search operations our adjutant Lakhbinder was tasked to carry out taxi borne operations. On both these occasions one terrorist each was killed. On 1 May some officers including the second in command Maj Harbans suggested that instead of starting an early morning operation it would be a good idea to start at night and ensure no movement in and out of the village for the complete night. The first target selected was a village near Kulgam. We cordoned it at about last light. Later around midnight the CO QRT while moving through the village saw some suspicious movement in one of the houses. It was quickly surrounded, we closed in and before we pressed the trigger we decided to peep through the door and were aghast to see Harbans and some of our boys inside. We thanked God that we didn't open fire otherwise we would have landed up with a serious problem. Things went off well. There was no militant activity that night. The CO QRT later located a fodder shed and spent the remaining night in it. This was a good experience for the CO to share the night with few officers and men on the grass in a 'kutcha' shed.

In the morning we got the menfolk together. After about three hours of effort we found that the search was turning in to a drab exercise. It was then, while going around the village we found a taxi and we decided to do something that had not been tried before. Luckily we also found the driver of the vehicle who was sitting in the cordon. Lakhbinder was tasked to take four boys in this taxi for about five km and to see if they could locate someone. He readily agreed. One understood the risks involved in an operation of this nature. There was a chance of the patrol getting overpowered. Therefore he was specifically told to go no further than five Km so that if required we could quickly react and reach him. We kept our fingers crossed.

About ten minutes later while the patrol had just crossed the next village they found a terrorist merrily walking along the road with an AK rifle slung on his shoulder just like a regular soldier. Sensing trouble, the moment the taxi stopped the terrorist took up a firing position and fired on the patrol. The fire was promptly returned. The militant was quickly neutralized. The CO QRT immediately joined up with the Adjutant, but before the CO could reach him the operation was already over. That was an excellent effort by Lakhbinder, Nek Singh, Shamsher and Diley Ram. Two more similar operations were successfully carried out in the following week.

It was after these operations that the terrorists stopped moving around carrying weapons freely in our area. On the contrary we were emboldened and started using buses, taxis, matadors and even horse carts (tongas) for our operations. We also got four burqas stitched. Four tailors of Prisal village were ordered to immediately take up the stitching of these burqas. However these were deliberately not collected immediately. The word spread in our complete area. Our Divisional headquarters picked up a message of banning of burqas for the complete south Kashmir for three months. These were however not used but it definitely created a scare in the minds of the militants. In the next few days we had extra ordinary operations on the 5,9 and on 12 and 21 May which are being discussed separately later in the text.

On 12 May we went to our regular hunting grounds of the Tral Valley. In order to achieve surprise we did not use service transport. We crossed the Vishwa river at three places that is, at Kaimuh, Arwani and at Sangam. We requisitioned matadors and raided the entire valley of Tral. Each officer led a QRT. Lakhbinder and Ashish rescued a young boy from the clutches of militants near Village Pastuna. Our commander joined us at Nanar and personally saw the boys chasing some suspicious persons up the Nanar hills who managed to get away. Dejectedly we came down, shared a quick bite with the Commander and then planned a raid into Tral town from two directions. Of the two different routes Harbans volunteered to take the longer and circuitous one while the CO took the shorter and straight route through the fields and over some streams and Nalas.

The patrol led by the CO crossed Aripal nala north of Nanar over a log bridge. Just before our leading scout was to step on the log bridge a dark snake 7 to 8 feet long also decided to do exactly the same. It suddenly appeared out of the bushes and crawled on to the log. We did not disturb it and let it pass. Some boys said it was a good omen while a few others said it was not. Nevertheless we decided to continue and concentrate on our immediate task ahead. The first village that we entered was Arigam which lies about two Km due west of Tral. No sooner did we enter the village there was some unusual activity. We saw some boys running in the village. We started running too and chased one group, caught a few boys, found them innocent, came back and chased another group. This time there was no mistake.

The group suddenly opened up with automatic weapons. The fire was returned and we started the chase breaking up into smaller groups. While one group led by Rifleman Rajeshwar Singh ran directly behind, Shamsher Singh with his buddy ran from the left (from the western direction), the CO with three boys chased them from the right (i.e. from the eastern direction). We managed to close in with two of the militants who were desperately firing in our direction. One bullet unfortunately hit Rifleman Rajeshwar on left of his waist. Almost simultaneously before he fell he managed to drop one militant dead. Meanwhile Lance Naik Shamsher

Singh closed in from the left while the CO did the same from the right. The second militant did not stop firing even though he was challenged by Shamsher and the CO and his buddy. At that moment Shamsher realized that his magazine was empty. Emboldened the militant fired at him. Having been surrounded the militant could not react fast enough which gave enough time to Shamsher to change his magazine and to finally finish the job. We recovered two AK rifles.

We lifted Rajeshwar, loosened his clothing and gave him some water to drink. That was the only thing he asked for. The Brigade Major was immediately contacted for arranging his evacuation by helicopter. A few minutes later we cancelled our request, the brave boy was leaving us for good. Before the Commander or others including Harbans, Ghanshyam, Amit [the RMO] could join us, Rajeshwar had gone. He had fought bravely and did us proud with his gallant action. He was very aptly awarded a Shaurya Chakra posthumously on the eve of Republic Day in January 1994.

Our operations in Tral valley on 12 May did not finish so early that evening. Before we could break up we learnt that a large number of residents living in Naner village had been warned to leave the area. They had packed their belongings in preparation to leave that night. We decided to intervene. While Harbans volunteered to stay back with a small patrol, the rest of us returned to the Brigade headquarters at Malangpura for a short break. On arrival there we learnt that our commander while returning from Tral had intercepted a taxi from where his QRT recovered two AK rifles. At nightfall the CO QRT with one company returned to Tral valley and linked up with Harbans and his patrol. We met representatives of the residents and assured them of our help. They changed their mind, sought a compromise with their neighbours and are happily still there.

Nine days later we had a historic encounter in which we apprehended Sheikh Abdul Aziz with 10 bodyguards from village Nilura in Pulwama district. The CO met the Commander in the evening on 20 May in his HQs. The Commander asked the CO to plan a good operation and try and nab a large group which was reportedly moving around in that area. This area was the responsibility of 11 RAJ RIF which had been moved to Sopore in April that year. Since the unit was not there, the militants thought they could move around freely. We therefore decided to address the village of Nilura which was away from the road and not easily accessible. 22

Grenadiers was also planning to address the same village but since we informed the Brigade Major first, the operation came to us. We started at 0200 h on 21 May, crossed the Rambihara River over a log bridge and cordoned the village by about 0430 h. The road bridge at Wachi had been damaged by the militants which forced us to use a log bridge. Our second in command Harbans who was following the CO nearly slipped and would have fallen in to the river. However the Gods were with us and he is safe and sound.

Inside the village there was tremendous unusual activity, people were running around. Some militants fired on our troops. There was a quick firefight in which two militants were injured, and Sheikh Abdul Aziz with 10 bodyguards apprehended. Fortunately there were no casualties to our troops. The news of the arrest of Sheikh spread like wild fire. The valley was ordered to be immediately shut down by the terrorists. The Commander and the General Officer Commanding 8 Mountain Division visited us in our operational area and complemented the boys for the good job that they had done. Brigadier A S Khanna, VrC was particularly very happy since he had told the CO to plan this operation only about 12 hours earlier.

The operation resulted in the recovery of eight weapons. During the month of May we had killed nine militants, apprehended 12 and recovered a total of 18 weapons. These included 15 AK rifles and three pistols. We also received a complimentary message each from the Chief of Army Staff and from the Army Commander. There were two messages from Brigadier SPS Kanwar, VSM the 31 Sub Area commander under whom we had operated till January that year. He had opted us out of Srinagar in preference to 6 Maratha Light Infantry Battalion. All these messages gave us greater inspiration in carrying out our duties in the service of the Nation.

OPERATION NILURA--ARREST OF SHEIKH ABDUL AZIZ

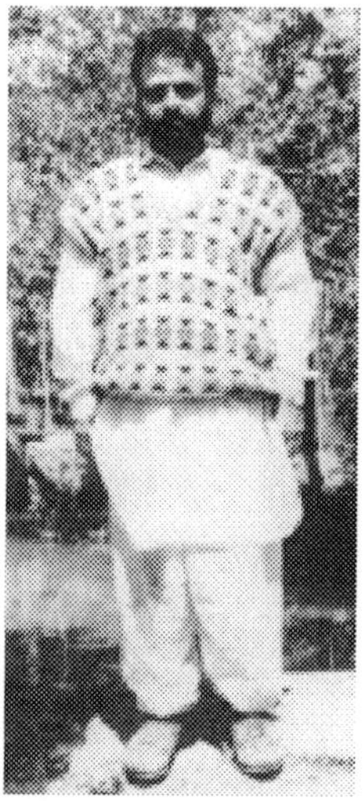

Sheikh Abdul Aziz, Supreme CDR, AL-Jehad

Bodyguards of Sheikh Abdul Aziz (less two evacuated to hospital)
OP Nilur – 21 May 1993

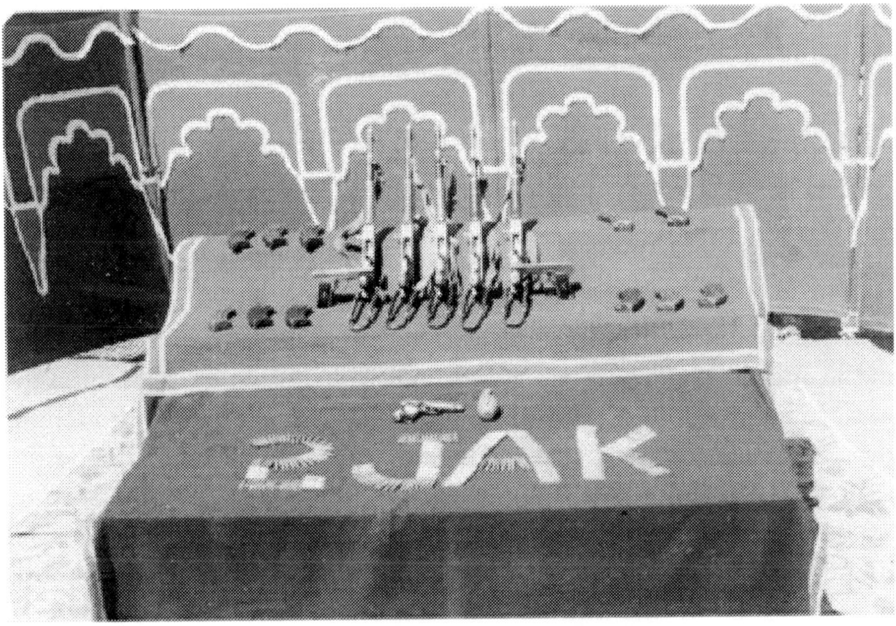

Recoveries OP Nilura – 21 May 1993

The next month of June 1993 passed off peacefully. The terrorists in and around our area decided to lie low for some time. On the night of 2 June which happened to be the marriage anniversary of the CO, we carried out an unsuccessful operation in area of Sonarwain in search of Mohammad Yusuf Shah alias Syed Salhuddin, the supreme commander of Hizbul Mujahideen. The activities of militants had otherwise decreased and so were their attacks on our camps. A few days later in a daring action Bravo Company under Major M Jogdand raided the village of Damal Hanjipura on 14 June. The company commander personally shot down a terrorist who dared to fire at the raiding party. Harbans was officiating as commanding officer and he led the daring patrols into the jungles of Damal Hanjipura. Before the month wound up, Harbans nabbed a platoon commander from village Khilan Gund near Nyuana in Pulwama tehsil.

June 1993 also saw the induction of 39 Infantry Division in to our sector. 87 infantry Brigade was assigned to replace us in our brigade sector while we prepared to move to Safapura near Manasbal Lake on Srinagar-Shalateng-Bandipur axis. We were tasked to initially train 2 GUARDS, then commanded by Col (Later Lieutenant General) Vinod Chopra for the role and tasks that we were performing. A number of lectures and joint operations were conducted. This incidentally was the second battalion that we trained. Earlier we had also trained 114 Infantry Battalion [TA] in February 1993.

In those days we used to generally carry out one operation every alternate day. On 3 July 1993 our Commander directed us to carry out anti militant operations every day. We did not know that whether the orders for increased intensity in operations had come from higher headquarters or were the orders of our commander himself, we carried out these instructions to the best of our ability. There were some cases of indiscipline in the unit during the preceding fortnight which could have also been the cause of increased intensity of operations. Next day was Sunday. Both units that is 2 JAK and 2 GUARDS had their morning prayers in their respective temples and at about 1000 h, half heartedly rushed for a day light cordon and search of village Yaripura, a notorious village about six Km from our unit. Villagers were totally taken by surprise since they were not expecting us to come out at that time and on a sunday. While rushing through the streets Captain Lakhbinder Singh encountered two terrorists, in a quick firefight he shot one while the other took refuge in a double storeyed house close by.

The operation lasted for five hours. We made numerous offers to the holed up militant to surrender which he refused. He was a notorious criminal code named Bilal and was not from Yaripura. Both commanders that is Brigadier A S Khanna, VrC and Brigadier M N Yadav commander 87 Infantry Brigade arrived on the scene. In their presence, efforts were again made to seek Bilal's surrender but he did not agree. Later we learnt that he was a company commander and our experience told us that such appointment holders generally did not succumb to pressure tactics. In the ensuing fire fight the house caught fire and Bilal jumped out from a first floor window. He was immediately received by a hail of bullets from a number of weapons that covered every corner of the house. He was killed instantaneously. At the same time a number of militants were picked up from among the congregation of the menfolk that we had collected in the open fields of the village by both units. The militants who were picked up surrendered one AK rifle and a grenade launcher to 2 GUARDS while we recovered two AK rifles from the two dead terrorists. Harbans unfortunately was injured in this action and had to be hospitalized for two weeks.

Two days later in another encounter near Bogund on Kulgam-Qaimuh road Major Paramjot Singh Virk was injured. He was officiating company commander of A company. On arrival at the village we saw some suspicious looking men at a distance of about a km. They were probably terrorists but did not appear to be armed. Though we ran after them for nearly two km they managed to get away, while we missed the militants we also had the unfortunate incident of injury to Major Paramjot. He was hit by five bullets on his right shin bone, an injury that he carries till date. We returned almost empty handed. Some of the boys were able to locate a militant hideout in the open fields from where we recovered some blankets and sleeping bags used by them. These items were later distributed to labourers working near Prisal. The operation upset all of us. In the past three days, operations had not gone very well. Two senior officers were injured and were out of action, fortunately for a short duration only. In addition we strongly felt that the recoveries made by 2 GUARDS on 4 Jul in Yaripura, rightly belonged to us since they were under training and had accompanied us only for a practice cordon and search operation. This incidentally was the first recovery of 39 Infantry Division therefore we decided not to make an issue out of it.

We were to leave Prisal in four days. While one company moved out on 7 July as advance party in preparation for the move of the main body, we decided to strike once again on 8 July. It was raining that day. Some of our colleagues recommended that we call off the operation but we decided to go ahead and in fact decided to strike deep towards the southern end of our area of responsibility. The target selected was the area of Khih Jogipura-Harman which lies well south of Yaripura. It was a two company operation led by CO QRT. Captain Lakhbinder and Lieutenant Ashish Maini did a commendable job. We approached the objective area from four different directions by day right through the rain and surprised the militants. Three of them were sitting on the banks of a stream busy having a pleasant conversation and were quickly nabbed. After a brief interrogation each one of them separately told us that they were from village Harmon and they had their weapons kept securely in the village.

We quickly moved to Harmon where we found to our pleasant surprise that 22 Grenadiers, our sister battalion was already carrying out a cordon and search operation. Two of our militants picked up their contacts from the congregation who quickly handed over one AK rifle each. The third militant took us to the fields from where he took out his AK rifle that was buried in the ground neatly wrapped up in a plastic cover. In two hours the operation was over. We assembled our boys near Kadir where we had a hot lunch of chana-batura in rain and thereafter returned to Prisal. This was the encouraging end of our first four months of our stay in this sector. Though two of our officers were convalescing in the hospital in Srinagar cantonment and Rifleman Rajeshwar Singh had been martyred in action, we had undoubtedly done our bit. The area had registered a loss of almost 50 terrorists together with their weapons. A substantial dent in the level of militancy had certainly been made.

CHAPTER 3

Shift to North Kashmir

We moved to North Kashmir on 10 July 1993 and were located astride the beautiful Manasbal lake near Safapura. This village lies midway between Shalateng which is on NH 1A and Bandipur, about 25 km from either town. Bandipur town lies along the northern bank of Wular lake about 50 km from both Shalateng and Sopur. The road rings around the great lake which is dominated all along by hills north of the line Safapura–Watlab located 10 km north of Sopur on the western bank of the lake. Watlab incidentally is located on the base of a feature housing the remains of the great Baba Shamsudin Sahib. The high features all along the road enabled the militants to pick up movements of approaching troops and vehicles which gave them adequate time to move deeper and higher into the numerous valleys thus successfully avoiding the troops whenever we tried to go after them. The hills dominating the northern banks of Wular lake provided adequate routes for movement of terrorists from Kupwara over Nachna Pass and from northern gullies in Kanjalwan Sector. The terrorists could either move to Sopur–Baramula and then to Badgam or via Ganderbal to Srinagar or to Pulwama/Anantnag. In other words this was a rich area for our task ahead. The battalion therefore occupied routes frequented by the terrorists which brought us into an unavoidable contest for domination.

On arrival we were tasked to carry out anti terrorist operations in three tehsils, two of Baramula district that is Sonawari and Bandipur and Ganderbal tehsil of Srinagar district. We took over the responsibility of the complete

Deployment of 2 JAK RIF in Bandipur Sector July 1993

brigade since the other two battalions were to join the formation about a month later. The Brigade headquarters and the battalion were co-located for the first time. We took two days to settle down and the next two days to learn about the terrain, its people and of course about our friends who had turned anti-national.

OPERATION KAITSON

On 14 July our commander planned Operation Kaitson a two battalion operation involving 11 RAJ RIF and us. 11 RAJ RIF was still located near Sopur where they had gone three months earlier. The plan involved our battalion to move around Wular lake through Bandipur and then to establish stops on the features astride Aloosa located along the northwest corner of Wular lake. 11 RAJ RIF was tasked to move via Kupwara, climb up the hills from the west, sweep across Nachna Pass from west to east and finally move down to Kaitson. Incidentally eight days earlier 10 BIHAR whom we relieved in Safapura had carried out a successful operation in the neighbouring area of Aloosa-Malangam.

The move involved covering 40 Km of open stretch all along the eastern bank of Wular Lake where it was difficult to hide large scale movement of service vehicles. We therefore brought two civil trucks to the unit in the evening, which were parked on the road under observation of the public and civil traffic. They were however parked facing southwards indicating as if they were headed towards Srinagar and not in the intended direction which was exactly the opposite. Our part of the operation involved moving two companies in civil trucks at midnight and occupying heights astride Aloosa-Kaitsan by first light and blocking escape routes of the terrorists hiding in the area. Later the battalion less two companies was to carry out a sweep, through Aloosa moving east to west and raid Kaitson from east. 11 RAJ RIF at the same time was to move west to east across Nachna Pass down to Kaitson.

The Brigade commenced moving at last light on 14 Jul 1993. 11 RAJ RIF moved out first. Our two companies boarded the trucks, turned them around and left the camp at Manasbal at midnight as planned. They were in position four hours later. We started at 0300 h followed by our commander and arrived at Aloosa at 0600 h. On arrival we quickly got down, deployed ourselves and commenced our sweep. Halfway up the valley near Belipura we heard the gunfire. We later learnt that a group of terrorists had indeed seen us and taken to their heels. They tried to escape through Belipura and through the Nalas located south of the village. Vigilant boys under our young officers challenged them first before getting engaged in a fire fight. The terrorists responded with full fury of automatic fire. The CO QRT immediately divided itself into three groups one each under the CO, Adjutant and the third under Captain C M Singh, the medical officer and closed with the militants. One of the militant pretending to be injured, shouted for help and requested for acceptance of his surrender. Lance Naik Naresh Kumar of C company decided to close in. No sooner had he stepped out of his cover that the militants fired at him. The brave man that he was Naresh almost at once not withstanding his injuries closed in with two of the terrorists and killed them before succumbing to his injuries. The medical officer joined up with Charlie company whose gallant effort resulted in elimination of seven 7 terrorists. One terrorist managed to injure Naib Subedar Kartar Singh, Rifleman Joginder Kumar and Rifleman Ghanshyam. This militant then ran and took refuge in a lone hut. This hut was immediately surrounded from three directions. Towards the east of the hut was a hill feature about 150 feet high. The CO and five other ranks climbed the feature so as to surround the terrorist. He was duly warned to surrender but he did not. We thereafter brought down accurate fire using rifles, light machine gun and later with a grenade launcher. The militant occasionally fired back. He was obviously trying to conserve his ammunition.

After about a dozen rounds of RL were fired and the hut nearly opened up from all directions, there was pindrop silence. We thought that the terrorist was dead and decided to close in to check. The CO with his patrol came down from the hill. As we were about to enter the house the militant fired again, he was very much alive. We ducked for cover and took up firing positions again. The fire fight continued. The terrorist was determined to fight it out, it was quite obvious that he was an appointment holder and not from the rank and file and therefore we needed extra effort to eliminate him.

The fire fight lasted four hours before the militant was finally neutralised. He was indeed a hardcore terrorist and a determined man. To our pleasant surprise he turned out to be the deputy commander in chief of Hizbul Muzahideen the most violent terrorist organization in the Kashmir valley. He was also the North Kashmir district commander. His code was Wafadar Khan. He had the distinction of participating in the Afghan war for 10 years and was known to be the right hand man of supreme commander of Hizbul Muzahideen, Yusaf Shah alias Syed Salaudin. Alongwith the district commander his deputy, Abdul Majid Sheikh was also neutralised. There were a total of 8 terrorists killed in this action. To this list, one more terrorist was added when some of the terrorists tried to engage our patrol tasked to evacuate the injured soldiers to Bandipura helipad. This encounter took place near Turkpura.

With the elimination of nine militants we recovered five AK rifles, 16 Magazines and 279 rounds of live ammunition. Maj Gen R S Mavi, AVSM, SC visited us that day for the third time in the operations and had a field lunch with us. He was particularly happy since he had launched a number of operations to neutralize this militant in the previous six months. He conveyed his condolences for Rifleman Naresh and complemented the unit for the excellent operation. We received a complimentary message from the General officer Commanding in Chief Northern Command. The entire Bandipura tehsil closed down for three days on the call of the terrorists for the second time in the month. They had earlier closed for the same period after the successful operation by 10 BIHAR REGT. This practice of closing shops was to continue for a number of times during our six months stay in the area.

There was a lull for the next four days before we struck again. The second operation was a lightning raid conducted in the area of Turkpura where the militants had tried to interfere in our evacuation effort on 15 July. This operation has been explained separately. Once again we were able to eliminate five more terrorists forcing the shopkeepers (on the call of the terrorists), to close down their shutters once again for the third time in the same month.

Six days later that is on 26 July 1993 General BC Joshi, PVSM, AVSM, Chief of Army Staff visited our unit. This visit was a singular honour for all of us to have our "Chief" amidst us in the operational area. He was accompanied by the following senior officers:-

(a) Lt Gen DSR Sahni, PVSM, SM, GOC-in-C Northern Command.
(b) Lt Gen Surrinder Singh, AVSM, GOC-in-C designate Northern Command.
(c) Lt Gen V R Raghvan, UYSM, AVSM, Director General Military Operations.

(d) Lt Gen (Later General & COAS) S Padmanabhan, VSM, GOC 15 Corps.
(e) Maj Gen K S Sethi, MGGS, Northern Command.
(f) Maj Gen R S Mavi, AVSM, SC, GOC 8 Mountain Division.
(g) Col T S Hassanwalia, Officiating Commander 81 Mountain Brigade.

The entourage came in five helicopters; the Safapura ground was big enough to accommodate them. 11 RAJ RIF our sister battalion was tasked to provide security to the campus and to the visiting dignitaries. Their taking over of the security enabled us to concentrate on the various other aspects of the visit. General B C Joshi, PVSM, AVSM, ADC had taken over as Chief of Army Staff on 1 July 1993 and this was his first visit to the J&K valley.

Vis of Gen B C Joshi, PVSM, AVSM, ADC Chief of Army Staff on 26 Jul 1993

The COAS visited the unit for an hour and a half that day. He was received by the CO and & SM and introduced to the unit officers and JCO's. Thereafter for about half an hour he was briefed on some of the important and successful operations carried out by the unit. Col T S Hassanwalia later told us that with the visit of the 'Chief' to any unit or a formation, one either makes it or one is doomed for ever. In our case he told us that the 'Chief' was extremely appreciative of the performance of the unit and complemented all ranks of the unit for its outstanding performance. He had tea with the troops and complemented all ranks for their operational performance and dedication. As per our practice we closed the festivities by proudly opening a bottle of champagne in the evening. We also thanked all ranks of the unit for their valour and sacrifice.

Before the month closed we were picked up for another very important task. This was to provide security to thousands of pilgrims visiting the holy shrine of Baba Amarnath. Colonel (later Brigadier) T S Hassanwalia our Deputy Brigade Commander called us up at about 2200 h on the 29 Jul and told us to take a three coy column to secure the area between Panchtarni and the Bhavan and to ensure safe passage for the pilgrims. CO was offered a helicopter flight the next day but the unit was to leave immediately so that it could be effective by first light on 30 July. We felt it was better to leave alongwith the unit that night itself. The flight was politely refused. We marched off at midnight and reached Sonamarg at 0500 h where we left our transport. After a quick wash we started our climb up via Baltal on to Panchtarni and the shrine. After a five hour climb we were all positioned in our respective locations by mid day.

Amarnath is a Hindu shrine in the Kashmir valley dedicated to Lord Shiva and located at an altitude of 3888 meters (12756 feet). The Shrine is 141 km from Srinagar. It is accessible via Anantnag-Pahalgam and also via Srinagar–Sonamarg-Baltal on the Srinagar-Leh axis. The first route starts from Pahalgam and is motorable till Chandanwari and thereafter there is an animal transport (AT) track all the way to Seshnag-Panctarni-Sangam and thereafter to the holy shrine. It is a 40 km three day walk to the shrine.

The second route starts from Baltal. The track leads to Sangam and then to the holy shrine, it is about half the distance. There is an AT Track now available but in 1993 this was only a foot track. While the route via Pahalgam takes a five day turnaround time however on the Baltal route it is possible to make it up and down in one day. This route however was extremely treacherous and difficult. One was required to walk up the steep slopes with the icy cold, light blue coloured waters hundreds of feet down below.

The Amarnath shrine is considered to be one of the holiest shrines by Hindus. It is surrounded by snow capped mountains. The cave itself is covered with snow during most of the year. It is open to the public for a short period of about two to three months. Inside the 40 meter high cave a stalagmite is formed by the freezing of waterdrops that fall from one corner of the roof to the floor. The ice block that forms takes a shape of a Shiva lingam as the Hindus believe. There are generally two more ice formations, they represent Parvati and Shiva's son Ganesha. Here Lord Shiva is believed to have explained the secret of life and eternity to Parvati. While Parvati is believed to have slept, two white pigeons probably heard the complete sermon. People believe they are still alive. Though this cannot be verified but it is true that white pigeons are there in the holy cave. They stay between the various folds and cuts within the walls and the roof of the cave. There can or rather must be more than two, but that is not certain however what is true is that they are definitely there. We all saw them.

Hindus have been known to be undertaking the holy pilgrimage to seek the blessings of Lord Shiva since time immemorial; however in the Middle Ages somehow the practice was discontinued. In the 15th century the cave was rediscovered by a shepherd of the Malik caste whose descendents get a portion of the earnings to this day. The holy pilgrimage has thereafter continued every year till it was temporarily closed by the militants in 1991-92. In 1993 it was decided to resume the pilgrimage and hence this deployment of 2 JAK RIF and 22 Grenadiers which was deployed on the Pahalgam route.

We were deployed for providing security to the pilgrims for a week. Besides seeking blessings from Lord Shiva we with his blessings provided cover to over a lakh and thirty thousand pilgrims that passed through our area during that period. The entire duration remained incident free. We voluntarily managed the 'darshan' with the help of bubbling youngsters ably led by R S K Nair and Hardeep. Our boys remained continuously inside the shrine for hours at a stretch and ensured that everyone got an opportunity to be with the gods for sometime. The people were happy, the Gods appeared happy too; but the sadhus and priests resented our presence for it meant cutting in to their income due the orderliness that the army ensured. They were forbidden to fleece the pilgrims.

We were visited by Commander 1 sector Rashtriya Rifles under whom we were deployed, the Honourable Governor, General (Retired) K V Krishna Rao, Lt General M A Zaki, Lt Gen Saklani, both advisors to the state government, Mr. B S Bedi, the Director General Police and Deputy Commissioner of Anantnag, Mr. Bhat. Accompanying the Governor was Dr Sudhir S Bloeria who later retired as a State Chief Secretary. Dr Sudhir S Bloeria also informed us that he himself had been commissioned in 2 JAK RIF some 25 years earlier and therefore was part of our unit. This was a wonderful piece of news. We also learnt that another officer of his seniority Shri Raj Mohan Vohra had joined the IAS in the mid Seventies and was posted as Commissioner Garhwal Division in Dehradun. It was good to establish contacts with our veterans whom we could approach for guidance and blessings. The operation brought us a message from GOC 39 Infantry Division who complimented all ranks for the good work they had done despite having moved without warning and operated in high altitude area without acclimatization.

We returned on 7 August to the beautiful fields of Safapura which we learnt were actually the grounds of a sheep farm. It was for this reason that the terrorists and the local populace began to call us 'sheep farm fauj (army)'. The drive against terrorists started once again with even greater vigour having been blessed by Lord Shiva. In the same month we recovered a total of six weapons. Though we apprehended two very important terrorists, 'Malik–a battalion administrator of Hizbul Mujahideen who gave us one AK 56 rifle and another one from a village called Wakura who gave us two weapons but the most interesting and daring operation was conducted by our Adjutant and Ashish Maini with a handful of youngsters. They carried out a daring raid in village called Bunyari located near the banks of Wular Lake. The total strength taken by these two brave officers was just a section of 10 boys. They managed to deceive all the villagers before reaching Bunyari. They crossed the water channel and surprised the terrorist guarding the crossing. After a brief firefight the terrorist was neutralised.

On the same day a brigade size operation was launched in the area of Erin bowl which incidentally yielded nothing. We had also experienced that whenever we went out of Safapura for operations in farflung areas the terrorists in and around Safapura had a field day to roam freely wherever they wanted. It was for this reason we decided to leave a small patrol duly supported by Subedar Faiju Ram with a QRT to deal with such terrorists, This gave us quick results that day. Incidentally the Commander also complimented the unit for quickly moving out a column immediately on return from the Brigade operation at about 8.30 pm. We were able to return to the comfort of our beds by about midnight that day, ready to be launched for the next operation.

On I September 1993 the command of our Division changed. Major General R S Mavi, AVSM, SC, the General officer Commanding 8 Mountain Division proceeded on posting to Senior Command wing at College of Combat (now called War College) a day earlier. He was replaced by Major General S S Grewal, SM, VSM of our regiment who was later to become our Colonel of the Regiment. On 2 September we carried out an operation in village Safapura from where we recovered two weapons. The month of September climatically is the best period of the year in the valley. This is the month when the valley is full of fruits. Almonds and walnuts start coming in to the markets and the fields are full of apples. They add to the beauty of the fields and the damsels. Unfortunately for us we dared not look or stare at them lest we lose our concentration. In happier times one could stop one's vehicle and share greetings and hopefully could expect a smile in return, but that was not to be now. Bad luck for all of us, youngsters and old alike. We disciplined ourselves to look straight over the men and the ladies, looking for our friends, the anti national elements, always ready to take action against them. This policy paid us well with the blessings of Durge Mata. Many a times we were able to outsmart the militants and were able to nab or eliminate them.

The beautiful month though passed off peacefully but we were able to add to our tally of weapons and terrorists. Before we moved in to October we had an interesting operation at Kondabal our neighbouring village just across the Manasbal Lake. A group of three terrorists was neutralised. Details of this operation are being covered separately. This operation lasted nearly 24 hours. Just before it finished the GOC 8 Mountain Division visited the Brigade Headquarters which was co-located with the unit. The result of the operation with the blessing of 'Durge Mata' our regimental deity had a positive effect for the battalion and the brigade. The GOC complimented all of us for the good job done.

There were numerous operations conducted one after the other with tremendous successes. An absconding policeman who had joined the ranks of Hizbul Mujahideen was eliminated in the Ajas bowl. He had been appointed launching commander by the terrorist organization. That was another setback to the terrorists, we recovered two weapons from him, an AK rifle with ammunition and a Chinese pistol.

There were three major operations in October and November. The first was a successful encounter on 6 October in the hills northwest of Bandipur in the general area of Wanagam. In this operation the battalion neutralised 24 terrorists, thereby eliminating a complete group which was tasked to exfilterate to Pakistan occupied Kashmir and fetch weapons for putting up a fight in Sopur against the security forces. The operation is being described separately as also the next operation of Hazratbal which lasted from 16 October to 17 November 1993. Both operations brought us complimentary messages from Chief of Army Staff and from General Officer Commanding in Chief Northern Command.

We returned to Manasbal on 17 November ready to resume our task after a gap of one month. In the preceding month the entire Valley was on strike, life had come to a stand still. All shops and markets were closed; even the terrorists decided to take a break. Every one decided to wait and watch for the outcome of the standoff between the security forces and the terrorists holed up in the famous shrine. A day before we returned, our sister battalion that is 22 Grenadiers suffered a few casualties in Sumbal, a small town near Wular Lake. The militants threw a grenade at a three ton vehicle causing serious injuries to all occupants. There were three fatal and over a dozen injured. This adversely effected the morale of the unit. In a conference next day where we discussed the proposed plan for clearance of Sopore (or Sopur) town called OP SAHAYTA III. We noted that the BODYGUARDS were assigned to be reserve to the other two battalions. It appeared as if we had come too late for the operation.

Sopore is a beautiful town located on the south western end of the Wular Lake, known for its world famous apples. It is about 35 Km north west of Srinagar and 16 Km from Baramula which is the District Headquarters. Sopore is a trading centre and is surrounded by a large number of hamlets. The town was set up by King Avantiverman's irrigation minister Suyya in the eighth century. It took the name from the minister and was called Suyya-pur or in short Sopore. In 1947 this town was raided by tribesmen from Mehsud and Afridi tribes of the Pashtun region of North West Frontier Province on 22 October. In the early fifties the town saw rapid urban growth primarily due to locational advantage of being in the centre of the valley, its rich and fertile soil, which is good for agriculture, abundance of water potentially supportive for the rearing of a rich variety of fishes due to the proximity of Wular lake as also several forest resources.

Sopore became a focus of separatist activities and continues to be a highly politicized hotbed of separatist activity with frequent spontaneous protests and strikes. On 6 January 1993 some militants snatched a gun from a BSF jawan who went to draw water from a water source which was across the road opposite their post. In retaliation the BSF fired on some civilians as also on a matador carrying about 15 passengers to Bandipura. The local media reported that over 50 people were killed and more than 200 shops burnt in the exchange of fire with the militants. Some houses were also gutted. As a consequence, the BSF was withdrawn from most of the places inside Sopore. In April that year 192 Mountain Brigade launched an unsuccessful operation in which they lost an officer. 5 GUARDS was made responsible for operations in the area. Though they had numerous successful operations but by and large the state machinery failed to control the town. Therefore our formation was tasked to clear the town and open the Sopore-Bandipur axis by establishing four company sized BSF posts along this road. 11 RAJ RIF of our Brigade was moved to this area in April from Malangpura. Incidentally their moving out of Malangpura helped us to nab Sheikh Abdul Aziz.

With the induction of 39 Infantry Division in June that year 8 Mountain Division was concentrated in North Kashmir. The operation was delayed for two months due to the Hazratbal crisis. The militants understood these moves too. They planned to send a large column of about 25 militants to POK to make up their requirements of arms and ammunition. This group was fortunately eliminated by our unit on 6 October in operation Alpine Noose in which 24 of them were neutralised and accounted for.

We had made a representation to the Brigade Commander for interchanging of task with 22 GRENADIERS. Their task was crucial for the complete operation. Besides having suffered casualties two days earlier their Commanding Officer was on leave and so was the Commanding Officer of the third unit too. Our Commander was actually unhappy with us since we returned to Manasbal quite late the previous evening. He was worried that we could well have been attacked by the terrorists enroute. We learnt later that a hand grenade had indeed been thrown on the vehicle of the Commanding Officer. It missed the vehicle and did not explode. Fortunately for all of us we learnt of it well after a fortnight or so. Therefore the Commander's apprehension was not wrong.

The Commander agreed to change our task as recommended. We clearly understood the consequences and made special efforts to brief officers, JCO's and the troops and convinced them of the importance of the operation. All officers and JCO's fully supported our move. As per intelligence reports given by the local police, the number of militants could be anything from 150 to 2000. Before we left our camp we spent an extra minute to seek the blessings of 'DURGE MATA' which though our normal routine was however special that day. We understood that we were going to face determined opposition and that we might come back minus some of us. We prayed to the gods to help and guide us do our task to the best of our ability without over worrying for the expected casualties. We decided that the operation would be led by the CO QRT.

Of the two battalions 2 JAK RIF and 11 RAJ RIF that were tasked to enter the town of Sopore it was the responsibility of our unit to hit at the core of the town in the general area of the J&K Bank and the police station. The CO had recommended that since surprise was difficult it would be better to enter the town when it was extremely cold. It was therefore decided on our recommendations, that we would commence moving to the objective exactly at midnight on 26/27 November 1993.

The operation commenced as planned. We began our movement on 26 via Sangerwain the base for Kanjalwan sector. Around midnight when we disembarked from our vehicles near Sopore we immediately realized that the whole town appeared to be up already. Loudspeakers were glaring anti-national slogans, sounds of "Allah-o-Akbar" could be easily heard over the gun fire of UMGs that were firing into the air. Nevertheless we moved on. The unit encountered three delay lines where we exchanged heavy fire with the militants. Seven terrorists were killed and five AK 56 rifles recovered. The report of each terrorist casualty was given to the commander on wireless. We learnt later that the commander and the complete brigade staff was up and alert and so was the ADS, which was headed by a lady doctor. Every time the CO gave him a report of militant action, he missed a beat, fearing the next news would be of a casualty. At night we suffered one casualty.

Our brave Adjutant Lakhbinder was hit by a bullet on his left thigh. We tried to cheer him up by telling him that he would be received by the lady doctor in the ADS deployed north of the town. But while evacuating him, the patrol took him via the southern route leading to Baramulla. So he missed meeting the lady doctor that was his bad luck, but he received medical aid much faster and recovered in a few days. The task was very well carried out. We finished our task well ahead of our scheduled time. In the morning Rifleman Buddhi Bahadur of our unit who was tasked to stand as sentry behind a water tank was hit by a grazing bullet on the neck. Though he looked more serious than Lakhbinder he recovered even faster. There was a sniper shot fired at us which hit the grille of the iron gate of the police station behind which we were standing. God was kind and there were no more casualties in the entire formation. The conduct of the operation brought us yet another complimentary message from the General Officer Commanding in Chief Northern Command who comlimented the entire formation and 2 JAK RIF in particular for the excellent conduct of the operation. This message is shown below.

OPERATION 'OP SAHAYTA III (SOPUR)' 27 NOV 1993 MESSAGE FROM ARMY COMMANDER

CI Ops in the valley comma appreciation (.) *ref ops by 81 MTN BDE and 192 MTN BDE in SOPUR on Nov 27 (.)* ***GOC-IN-C comma NORTHCOMD complements all tps who participated in the above Ops particularly 2 JAK RIF*** *(.) Gen offr hopes that tps will continue to do their good work (.) all add*

OP Sahayta III, 27 Nov 1993 (Sopur)

The last month of the year brought in the usual chill in the air. Despite the lowering of temperatures the spirits of all ranks suddenly shot up with the receipt of a signal from Army Headquarters nominating the unit for an award of citation by the Chief of Army Staff. This was a singular honour for the unit. It could be equated to a battle honour that our unit last received in the First Great War almost 70 years earlier. It indeed was an occasion to rejoice, a good recognition for the hardwork of the previous one and a half year and the sacrifices made. We offered our grateful thanks to God Almighty and Durge Mata our unit Deity for their continued guidance and blessing.

All available officers, junior commissioned officers and men were collected and the Commanding Officer broke the news with moist eyes. All ranks were thanked for their hardwork and dedication which brought us this recognition from the Chief of Army Staff. All ranks present and past indeed deserved our grateful thanks. The Unit Citation was to be awarded by the Chief of Army Staff on 15 January 1994 on the occasion of the next Army Day in New Delhi. The Commanding Officer and the Subedar Major travelled to New Delhi to receive the same. For Subedar Major Roshan Lal, it was an event of greater importance for it happened only a month before he retired. He had become Subedar Major of the unit in 1989 a year that saw major sacrifices being made by the battalion in Sri Lanka during OP 'Pawan', things were bad then, morale was extremely low, the then Commanding Officer was prematurely moved out. This time things were good, morale was exceptionally high and the Commanding Officer and the Subedar Major were received by the Chief of Army Staff at the Army Day Parade on 15 January 1994.

CHAPTER 4

Redeployment in South Kashmir

The first day of 1994 saw us back in our old area of Malangpura-Panjgam. For about two and a half months the battalion was located at Panjgam near Malangpura: In mid March we were re-deployed in Prisal-Yaripura subsector. We occupied same posts that we had in 1993. We were tasked to operate in Prisal–Yaripura again since 39 Mountain Division was to move out of the valley after handing us our area again. We changed hands by 10 January and relieved 87 Mountain Brigade. Operations commenced in right earnest. On 15 January we received the unit citation from Chief of Army Staff, General B C Joshi, PVSM, AVSM, ADC, at the Army Day parade in New Delhi. It was extremely cold that day. There was dense fog and one could hardly see anything. It rained during the parade for a short while dropping temperatures further. We had a celebration in DSOI in New Delhi organized by Ghanu that was attended by Lieutenant General G L Bakshi, PVSM, Brigadier Romesh Gupta, Majors Sawhney, Avtar, Sundaram, Ghanshyam and Captains Lakhbinder and C M Singh besides the CO and his wife. Most officers were accompanied by their wives. We followed it up with another celebration at Panjgom, our unit headquarters on return where we once again opened another bottle of champagne. Army Day and Republic Day 1994 brought us numerous awards too.

Commanding Officer and Subedar Major receiving Unit Citation from General B C Joshi, PVSM, AVSM, ADC, Chief Of Army Staff on 15 Jan 1994

Reception at Army House 15 Jan 1994

CO & his wife with COAS & CO 4 JAK RIF

Celebration at DSOI with Lt Gen G L Bakshi PVSM Colonel of the Regiment on 16 Jan 1994

On Army Day while the CO and the SM were busy receiving the Unit Citation in Delhi the unit under Harbans, the Second in Command carried out an excellent operation in village Ashmuji which was again complimented upon by the GOC.

The tally of militants neutralised and weapons recovered kept constantly moving up. On February 8 once again we had a very interesting operation. Having split ourselves into small parties we raided a number of villages. Lakhbinder caught a terrorist in Nunmai village near Chittargam (Kashu) where Alpha company had stayed under Ghanshyam eight months earlier. While interrogating him, he got a lead and informed the CO who immediately left on a wildgoose chase while he himself kept working on the terrorist trying to motivate him to voluntarily give up the path of militancy. Reluctantly, the terrorist decided to hand over one weapon initially. He happened to be a company commander and we knew he had more. Slowly and deliberately the interrogation continued and out came a total of eight weapons including a sniper rifle. It was a fantastic job done by Lakhbinder. We did not mind the wild chase because our overall result at the end of the day was indeed very heartening. This operation again brought us complimentary messages from our commanders.

In the third week of the month, the CO and the Subedar Major attended the Biennial Conference and Sixth Reunion at Jabalpur. There were many senior officers of the regiment as also from our unit including Brig B K Agarwal, VSM, Cols D S Sandhu commanding 1 JAK RIF, D K Chaudhry commanding 20 JAK RIF, A B Patil, O P Singh and L S Sundram. All had good words and cheer for the unit. It felt most encouraging to speak to them.

Bodyguard Family

With BODYGUARD Veterans

The function finished with the reunion dinner in the Regimental Centre officers mess. To our pleasant surprise, Major General (Later Lt Gen) SS Grewal, SM, VSM our General Officer Commanding suddenly went up to the stage and announced that he had a special announcement, to make. Every one wondered as to what did he suddenly have up his sleeve. He announced that the BODYGUARD in a daring operation the previous day in village Lariyar near Dadsura in Tral valley had neutralised five foreign terrorists and recovered five weapons from them. Ghanshyam and Lakhbinder in the absence of the CO had done a magnificent job indeed. There were complimentary messages once again from Army Commander, GOC 15 Corps and from GOC 8 Mountain Division.

On 1 March Ghanshyam carried out yet another successful operation, this time in village Dadsura in Tral valley close to Lariyar where they had operated on 26 February. Three AK rifles were recovered and two Pakistan trained terrorists apprehended along with ammunition and explosives. In the next nine days, a series of successful operations were conducted which resulted in killing or capture of as many terrorists. The recovery of weapons was impressive too. One AK rifle was recovered on 4 March, one on 8, two on 9 and yet another on 10 March. GOC 8 Mountain Division sent us another complimentary message.

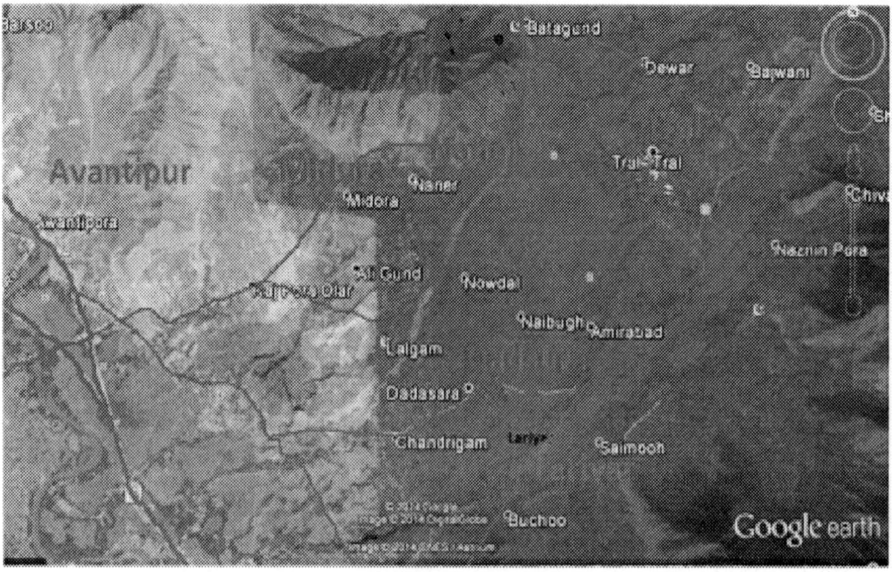

The Tral Valley

On 8 March we travelled from Panjgam to Prisal on our way to Yaripura. This village being congested we did not use our vehicles, instead we walked through it. Just outside the town we requisitioned a bus and drove to Bolus which was about a km away. Half way through, while driving past the village of Tarigam Payeen we saw a terrorist standing about 300 m away. An AK rifle on his shoulder was clearly visible. We deliberately did not react immediately but continued our drive to Bolus giving the impression of normal movement of a civil bus. At the Bolus crossroads we dismounted half of the CO QRT and sent them back to Tarigam Payeen on foot. The remaining CO QRT with the CO turned right and drove to an area south of Tarigam Payeen, the target village where the terrorist had been seen.

The terrorist saw the troops closing towards him. He ran south of the village where he encountered the CO's patrol which had already arrived by bus. At this stage the terrorist panicked and quickly fired a few rounds from his AK rifle. Realizing that he was surrounded and had no chance to escape, he threw his weapon and raised his hands. He was overpowered and his weapon and ammunition taken. We walked back through Yaripura. And once out of the village boarded our vehicles and returned to Panjgam.

In the week following we shifted back to our deployment of the previous year. While the Battalion Headquarters with two companies were located in Prisal, Charlie company was located in Mamman and Delta company in Zainapura. The first half of the battalion looked after the area along road Arwani-Yaripura-Kulgam and the remaining two companies dominated the area along the road Arwani-Zainapura-Shopian. This entire area was looked after by two battalions of our brigade, the northern portion by the BODYGUARDS and the southern by 22 GRENADIERS.

Immediately on arrival in Prisal one of the terrorists who had been apprehended earlier managed to dodge us by escaping from our custody at night from within the camp. It was indeed very shocking for all of us. We pulled ourselves up, improved our drills and vowed not to repeat such blunders. Fortunately there were none thereafter. In the next month we continued to dominate our area and made occasional forays into the Tral valley. Between the period 15 March and 18 April 1994, 16 terrorists were neutralised. These operations resulted in recovery of six weapons and a large quantity of ammunition and explosives.

The first quarter of the year had resulted in neutralization of 43 terrorists. There were six complimentary messages received which included two each from General Officer Commanding in Chief Northern Command, 15 Corps and from 8 Mountain Division. During the same period we had also received 18 awards on the occasion of Army Day and Republic Day in January. The awards included two Shaurya Chakras awarded to Late Rifleman Rajeshwar Singh and to Lance Havildar Nek Singh who was destined to stay with us for only a few more months.

The GOC-in-C sent us another message for our successful operation that was conducted on 4 April in Derapura near Kulgam.

25 April 1994 was the 126 Raising day of the unit, a day on which we solemnly paid homage to our brave soldiers who had over the years made the supreme sacrifice in service to the nation. We rededicated ourselves to the task at hand and decided to put in our best in the remaining period of our tenure in the valley. Three days later on 28 April we were involved in yet another operation that resulted in the elimination of two terrorists and recovery of one AK rifle and one pistol. The very next day two more terrorists were arrested which brought us one more AK rifle. This was followed by yet another recovery the very next day. Two Pakistan trained terrorists were eliminated in a village called Yemruch which lies on the outskirts of Yaripura. Of these two one was a battalion commander of Hizbul Mujhideen. We recovered one AK rifle and one pistol from the slain terrorists. A radio set was also recovered from them.

The month of May was once again very hectic. Our operations in this month resulted in the elimination of 15 terrorists belonging to Hizbul Mujahideen, Al Jehad and Muslim Janbaj tanjims of Pulwama and Anantnag districts. During this period 13 weapons were recovered. Successful operations were carried out on 3, 6, 7, 10 13, 16, 20, 21, 24, 28 h and on 31 May. There was a complimentary message from COAS for our operation in Anantnag on 3 May.

The successful conduct of operations during the past few days brought us an interesting message from the Brigade Headquarters on 7 May. This is a prized possession of the unit today and a copy is reproduced below. It clearly reflects on the performance of the unit during that period.

"Cdr has keenly obs your ops during past four days and deeply appreciates the offensive spirit in all rks of BODY GUARDS (.) wishing you successes in all your future endeavours (.) well done and keep it up"

(Commander has keenly observed your operations during the past four days and deeply appreciates the offensive spirit in all ranks of BODYGUARDS, wishing you successes in all your future endeavours, well done and keep it up)

In the next ten days six more terrorists were apprehended from whom 4 weapons including one AK rifle and three pistols were recovered. On 11 June the battalion neutralized four dreaded terrorists. That day we decided to carry out a sweep of area Paniyoh in Kulgam tehsil of Anantnag district. Moving in from six different directions in the afternoon, the move took the four terrorists in Paniyoh by total surprise. They were relaxing in the fields and were not expecting us at that particular time. We had with experience realized that it was best to keep changing our timings of operations. That day, it was because of this reason that we could surprise them. The terrorists on confrontation immediately took up positions and brought down heavy volume of fire on our troops. Our boys in an example of coordinated teamwork, determination, displaying better training and presence of mind, neutralized all the four terrorists after an intense firefight. They all belonged to Hizbul Mujahideen. We recovered four AK rifles with 12 magazines and 32 rounds of AK rifle ammunition. The operation as usual brought us complimentary messages from Division and Corps Headquarters.

On 20 Jun we had cordoned off village Khudwani in Kulgam tehsil of Anantnag District. The cordon was laid early in the morning and we delinked from the village at 1100 h after meeting no success. On the way back, one of our vehicles came under IED attack in which Subedar Faizu Ram and four other boys of Charlie Company received minor injuries. The terrorists involved in the IED attack managed to escape to a village close by. We proceeded to Kulgam which is about 10 Km to the south and carried out a similar operation in that area. The battalion delinked from the area of operations at 1300 h and returned to its permanent location. While the rest of the battalion continued to move to the base at Prisal, the CO QRT along with Captain Amit Chatterjee, the Regimental Medical

Officer and Ghatak Pl under Major Lakhbinder Singh, SM using a civil bus and a truck raided the villages of Kaimuh and Khudwani at 1430 h for the second time on the same day. These were the same villages where we faced the IED attack in the morning. We managed to establish contact with one of the terrorists involved in the IED attack. In a quick fire fight the terrorist was eliminated. We recovered one AK rifle with two magazines with 33 rounds, six detonators, one battery and an electronic flash for IED detonation.

In the same month two more successful operations were carried out on 23 and 26 Jun. While on 23 a battalion commander of Tehrik-ul-Mujahidin was apprehended alongwith a pistol by 2/Lt R Tiwari and boys of Alpha Company. Three days later which happened to be birthday of our brave Adjutant Major Lakhbinder, SM, two Pak trained terrorists of Hizbul Mujahidin were neutralised by 2/Lt Vinay Shahi and boys of B Coy in village Harigram of Kulgam tehsil. One of these two terrorists was the dreaded company commander code Paley Khan of Hizbul Mujahidin. He had been responsible for number of attacks on us. A year earlier around the same time he had managed to elude us, this time however he met his end. GOC 8 Mtn Div sent us another complimentry message for the successful operation.

During the month we were visited by Lt Gen G L Bakshi, PVSM, ADC who was then our Col of the Regiment. He had promised us in February that year during the Regimental Reunion that he would definitely visit us before he hung up his uniform on 31 July 94. He stuck to his promise and paid us a visit in Prisal. He was extremely happy to see the boys performing so well. Before coming to the unit he had met the GOC 15 Corps in Srinagar who had given him a brief account of the performance of the unit. Lt Gen G L Bakshi, PVSM, ADC in his address to the troops complimented all ranks for their continued good performance and wished us good luck for the balance period of our stay in the sector.

One day around this time, in a conference of all officers we discussed the issue of our performance in the operations. We had done two years in the valley by then and had already been awarded a Unit Citation by the honourable COAS in January that year. We suggested to every one that we were then in a situation where we could, with continued hard work and blessing of 'Durge Mata' work for another Unit Citation. Such situations come very rarely in life and we must work in that direction. One has never been so ambitious but this was a situation that we could not let it pass without a fair attempt. All officers present in that conference readily agreed and promised to put in their best. They were also told that we will work with absolute sincerity as we had all along been doing in the tenure and that there won't be any undercutting, illegal or unfair things done that could tarnish the image of the unit.

On 4 July another Pakistan trained terrorist was neutralised by 2/Lt Vinay Shahi and troops of Alpha Company. Four days later Maj Lakhbinder Singh, SM and Captain Gulshan Chadha alongwith CO QRT apprehended two Pak trained terrorists of Hizbul Mujahidin and recovered two AK rifles and a revolver from them. On 9 July Major Lakhbinder Singh, SM and 2/ Lt R Tiwari alongwith troops of Alpha Company neutralised yet another terrorist of Hizbul Mujahidin and recovered one AK rifle. Next two days that is on 10 and 11 July three more terrorists were neutralized by 2/Lt Abhay Avasthi, Naib Subedar Jai Singh and the boys of CO QRT.

On 11 July Sub Bhag Singh and Sapper M Ganesh of 17 Engineer Regiment succeeded in detecting and disarming a powerful IED and thus nullified the likely damage to us. During the period 16 to 19 July our battalion in a series of actions recovered a large number of arms and ammunition both in Shupian tehsil and in Srinagar. While Captain Hardeep Singh was involved in recovery of 2 AK rifles on 16 July, on 18 and 19 July, Maj Lakhbinder Singh, SM and 2Lt Vinay Shahi alongwith CO QRT and troops of B Coy succeeded in apprehending a dreaded battalion commander of Al-Jehad in Srinagar city. The troops also apprehended a district commander of the same force. This was a shift operation carried out in the suburbs of 'Down Town' Srinagar from where a total of seven AK rifles and six 9mm pistols were recovered alongwith large quantity of ammunition. Once again we received complimentary messages Chief of Army Staff and from Corps and the Northern Army commander.

Major Ghanshyam Katoch who had spearheaded the operation as officiating commanding officer was aptly awarded a Commendation Card by the Chief of Army staff for conspicuous bravery, dedication and outstanding devotion to duty. During this period Lance/Naik Parma Chand of Charlie Company had suffered gun shot wound during operations in Tral Valley on 14 Jul 1994. With the grace of "Durge Mata" there was no serious damage and he soon recovered and rejoined the battalion for further operations.

On 15 Aug 1994 the battalion was awarded 11 awards which included one Shaurya Chakra, posthumously awarded to Lance/Naik Naresh Kumar, two Sena Medals, four commendation cards from Chief of Army Staff and another four from GOC-in-C Northern Command. While Captain Hardeep Singh was awarded Sena Medal, Maj Lakhbinder Singh, SM and Captain Gulshan Chadha were awarded a commendation card each by COAS. We also received two more commendation cards of GOC-in-C Northern Command awarded to Havildar Lekh Raj and to Havildar Nek Singh.

On the same day, at about 1400 h one of our brave soldiers Lance/Havildar Nek Singh, Shaurya Chakra who had been injured on 7 August succumbed to his injuries in the 92 Base Hospital. He had in a daring action on 7 August in village Turk Tashlu along the Vishwa river, neutralised two Pakistan trained terrorists resulting in recovery of one AK rifle with one magazine and five rounds and one hand grenade. He had been seriously injured in the firefight. Lance/Havildar Nek Singh was indeed a brave soldier having been awarded repeatedly for daring actions. Later he was also awarded Kirti Chakra, for his gallant action on 7 August 94. In recognition of his bravery and dedication the Regimental Centre Jabalpur aptly named a specially created lake in his honour and called it 'Nek Sarovar'. The loss of this brave soldier did result in a serious setback to the battalion, however, his enthusiasm and dedication urged us to continue to operate against the terrorists with added zeal and determination.

Three days later the Battalion neutralised seven Pakistani trained terrorists of Hizbul Mujahidin in village Kaimuh. This was also our favourite hunting ground since there were too many militants in that area. We repeatedly achieved successes from Kaimuh and surrounding villages. This time the operation lasted thirty six hours. During the period four dreaded terrorists including one district commander and one district administrator of Hizbul Mujahidin were neutralised. Three other terrorists were also apprehended. A total of three AK rifles with six magazines, 107 rounds of ammunition and one radio set were recovered. The successful conduct of the operation was duly complemented upon by number of senior officers including the GOC-in-C Northern Command.

On 31 Aug 94, we were visited by Major General SS Grewal, SM, VSM, GOC 8 Mountain Division who had recently taken over as our Colonel of the Regiment on 1 August of that year. He spent the night with us at our battalion HQ in Prisal. He complimented all officers, junior commissioned officers and troops for their bravery, dedication and devotion to duty displayed in anti terrorist operations in the valley which had resulted in award of 43 gallantry awards till that day. We were fortunate to be the first battalion visited by the General after having taken over the reins of the Regiment. In the preceeding week, operations of the battalion had resulted in neutralization of five Pakistani terrorists and recovery of two rifles and five magazines with 63 rounds of ammunition.

A day after the visit of the Colonel of the Regiment, the battalion once again succeeded in apprehending two terrorists. Next day that is on 3 Sep, Major M Jogdand with troops of Bravo Company succeeded in carrying out a successful operation in the general area Qadir (also called Yadir) near Panjgam which resulted in neutralizing four terrorists of Hizbul Mujahidin that included three Pakistani nationals and apprehension of yet another. A total of five weapons was recovered which included three AK rifles and two pistols, 17 magazines and 433 rounds of ammunition. Continuing at the same pace the CO QRT neutralised another terrorist on 4 Sep and one more rifle AK 56 was recovered from him. The GOC 8 Mountain Division once again sent us complimentary messages.

After 15 Aug 1994 when our brave Nek Singh succumbed to his injuries we had announced a cash incentive of one thousand rupees as award for each weapon recovered from any terrorist. This did reboot the morale of the troops. Operations conducted thereafter succeeded in eliminating a large number of terrorists belonging to various tanjims. With the blessings of Durge Mata we had no serious injury or casualty for about three weeks that is from 15 August to 6 September. On 7 September while operating in the area of Palno Panditpura which lies in Kulgam tehsil of Anantnag district, we succeeded in eliminating three Pakistan trained terrorists of Hizbul Mujahidin, but we lost four of our brave boys. In addition Captain Gulshan Chadha and one more boy was injured. The details of this operation have been described separately.

Briefly on this day once again we had decided to carry out a sweep of the area south of Yaripura late in the afternoon. We approached this area from four different directions and simultaneously commenced the sweep at about 1400 h. To achieve surprise our troops had used civil trucks and buses to approach the target area. During this period terrorists were known to be resting in apple orchards. They were once again taken by surprise. One of the terrorists managed to take cover in a three-storeyed house from where he managed to cause us all the casualties mentioned above. The three fatal casualties included Havildar Piar Singh, Rifleman Joginder Kumar, and Rifleman Phula Sherpa. Few days later while Captain Gulshan Chadha and Rifleman Kharak Bahadur were discharged from the hospital, Sub Omkar Singh Manhas succumbed to his injuries in the base hospital. This was a terrible loss that the battalion suffered in a single operation. Though this was very demoralizing nevertheless it increased our resolve to carry out our task with even greater zeal and dedication.

On 13 September General KV Krishna Rao, PVSM (retd), His Excellency the Governor of Jammu and Kashmir, in a grand function held at Raj Bhawan in Srinagar presented a silver salvor to the battalion for the outstanding performance of the unit in anti terrorist operations. This was a great honour bestowed upon the battalion by the Government of J&K. The Honorable Governor was extremely appreciative of the performance and the contribution of the unit. This was the second occasion in one year he had met and complimented the Commanding Officer.

In October that year the battalion kept up the tempo of operations against the terrorists. Fourteen terrorists were neutralised mostly belonging to Hizbul Mujahidin and Al-Jehad tanzims in Pulwama and Anantnag districts. The operations resulted in recovery of eight weapons including six rifles alongwith a large quantity of ammunition and other warlike stores. We also recovered two radio sets on 16 Oct which adversely effected the communication set up of the terrorists. On 30 Nov 94 two more Pakistan trained terrorists of Hizbul Mujahidin were neutralized in village Guchroo in Kulgam tehsil of Anantnag district. We recovered two more AK rifles with seven magazines and 165 rounds. This operation preceded the visit of Major General (later Lt Gen) GS Sihota, GOC Victor Force under whom the battalion had been placed temporarily with effect from 15 Oct 1994. During the visit he complimented all ranks for the successful conduct of operations in our area of responsibility. This was one of the first successes of Victor Force after it had been raised and operationalized.

Before the end of the year the battalion received orders to move to Pithoragarh as the next peace station. This however was subsequently changed to Sanjuwan in Jammu. The year had brought us number of successes, including large number of honours and awards, however, at an exceptionally high cost in terms of casualties. We had lost Sub Omkar Singh alongwith five other ranks in different operations. Two other boys, Lance/ Naik Cook Ram Chandra and Rifleman/Cook Kamal Kishore Shukla had departed in accidents while on leave. The boys had once again made tremendous sacrifices and displayed gallantry for which we ware awarded one more Unit Citation this time by GOC-in-C Northern Command. We were unofficially informed that it had been decided not to award a second Unit Citation by the COAS in one tenure of the unit. Nevertheless it was a grand recognition of the hard work displayed by all ranks of the unit in curbing terrorism in the troubled valley.

On 31 Dec 1994 we decided to carry out a daylight operation once again commencing in the afternoon in the general area of Yaripura and Chitargarm. These places were about 6 km south of our battalion location of Prisal and Zainapura. Though we had planned to terminate the operation well before last light and be ready to watch the change over of the Year on TV, however, it continued for nearly 28 hours. Instead of enjoying the new year watching TV in the mess tent, we were out in the open operating against terrorists with nearly one foot of snow in the area of Yaripura and

Bolus. Details of this operation are also being narrated separately. A total of three dreaded Pakistani terrorists of Hizbul Mujahidin including a company commander were neutralised in this operation from whom two AK 56 rifles were recovered. Operation was carried out by CO QRT with Captain Vinay Shahi as officiating adjutant and two companies. The young officer was unfortunately severely injured and had to be evacuated to the hospital. He had spearheaded the operation and personally eliminated the first terrorist. He unfortunately suffered loss of an eye, a loss which has not dampened his spirits.

The successful conduct of the operation was applauded by all commanders including the Chief of Army Staff, who in his personal message conveyed his congratulations for the conduct of this successful operation. During the month of January 1995 we received one more Sena Medal, and five commendation Cards from GOC-in-C Northern Command. The Sena Medal was awarded to Naik Pawan Kumar. A few days later, around 20 January Lt Gen S Padmanabhan (later General and COAS) General Officer Commanding 15 Corps had called the CO and Brig Prakash Gurung who had just taken over the command of 81 Mountain Brigade for an interaction. During the discussion he instructed us to carry out a fire fighting exercise in the village Larao Jagir which lies to the north of Tral. Larao Jagir had suffered extensive damage on 10 January 1995 at the hands of some troops of another battalion. He was visibly moved with the details of damage caused in the village. In a lengthy briefing of about 45 minutes with a cup of Kawa he asked the CO whether he could shift his battalion to the Tral Valley immediately. The General Officer Commanding 15 Corps knew all along, that with the snow on the roads, it was not possible to move vehicles with heavy baggage. The CO assured him that the move would be carried out as desired and the vehicles could be moved later. The responsibility was changed due to extreme confidence that the GOC 15 Corps had in the unit.

This move was carried out on foot and we assumed the responsibility of the new area before Republic Day. The GOC 15 Corps had clearly spelt out our task in Tral Valley. We were told to ensure that the village of Larao Jagir should be turned around in the next three months, from a state of hatred towards the security forces, to a friendly one. This was duly done and shown to the General Officer Commanding 8 Mountain Division within the stipulated period of three months. During the latter's visit to the village in April a representation from the villagers was received by the GOC requesting him to extend the tenure of the unit, which was fortunately not accepted.

During the historic meeting with the GOC 15 Corps in Badamibagh in January 1995, there was an interesting incident that needs to be mentioned. Towards the end of our nearly 45 minutes of discussion, the General Officer Commanding turned his attention towards Brigadier Prakash Gurung. He asked the commander a few general questions and thereafter asked him specifically if he had settled down. The Commander confidently said "yes he had". Out of the blue, he suddenly looked at the commanding officer who was sitting directly opposite him across the table and said, "has he". The CO was caught off guard and had to say "of course sir". There was no choice. But the damage was done. We knew that the commander did not like it. An innocent question by the General had suddenly created a problem for us. Notwithstanding the ripples created by this dialogue the unit worked hard and was hopefully able to overcome the misimpression created.

After the discussion with GOC 15 Corps we moved the battalion on foot to the Tral valley leaving behind a rear party to look after the heavy baggage. This was fetched up later after about 15 days when the snow melted on the roads. We deployed our Battalion less three companies in the area of the canal rest house in Tral and, of the three remaining companies, Bravo was deployed at Kral Chak from where the road takes off for Midura-Nanar from the Awantipur Tral road. This road to Midura continues to Pastuna and then to Wagad, where it connects to the Tral-Wagad road and there after continues to Satura. We deployed Delta company at Wagad and Charlie at RH canal, which dominated another route out of, Tral Valley. This deployment helped us to check movement of all personnel moving in and out of the entire Tral valley.

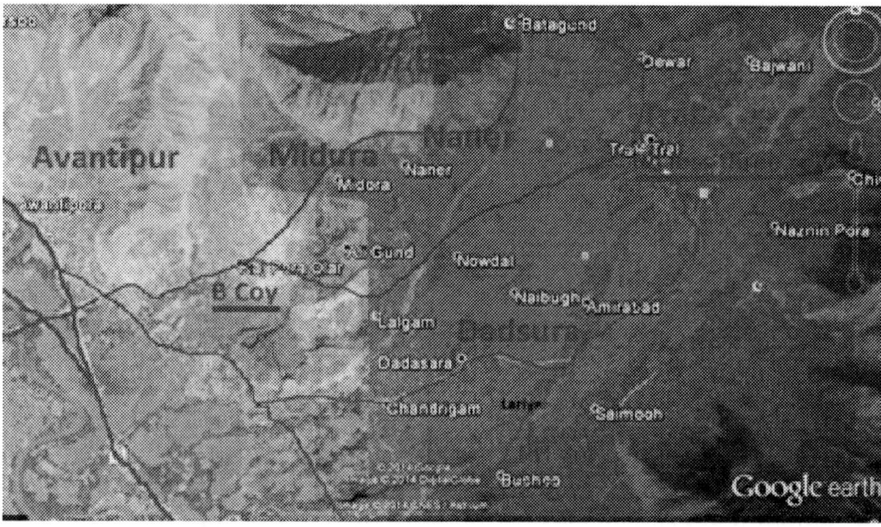

Deployment of 2 JAK RIF in Tral March 1995

Starting afresh in the Tral valley, on 7 and 8 March the battalion neutralised one terrorist from Afghanistan and apprehended two more belonging to Al-Umar tanzim. A total of five weapons was recovered which included one AK rifle and four pistols. Earlier one more pistol was recovered on 26 February in Midura. On 10 March 1995 a Pakistan trained terrorist was neutralised in village Turk Tashlu in Kulgam tehsil. He was a Battalion Commander of Hizbul Mujahidin and was responsible for carrying out IED attacks on the National Highway near Biz Bihara. He had been active for the past three years and had successfully carried out a number of IED attacks against many units including us. This was a chance encounter conducted by the CO QRT.

On that day the CO had by chance gone to Anantnag to meet the Deputy Commissioner and SSP Anantnag. On return we decided to take a route through our old area from Khanabal to Khudwani and thereafter along Vishwa River to Arwani which lies about three km south of Biz Bihara. This area had a large number of terrorists operating on both sides of Vishwa River. Short of Arwani there is a small village called Hasanpur Tabela which has a famous business house called "Rishi Carpets". In south Kashmir they were the only one involved in cutting and washing of carpets. The CO had given them a carpet for washing. There being undue delay in receipt of the carpet the CO had decided to visit that village on his return from Anantnag.

The Vishwa river was the boundary between 1 and 3 Sector Rashtriya Rifles. While 1 Rashtriya rifles was responsible for the area north of the river 3 Sector Rashtriya Rifles was responsible for the area south of the river. The terrorist staying along the river generally kept shifting depending upon which troops approached them. It was mid day by the time we reached that village. The terrorists, by then knew where the troops of both these formations were deployed. They were not expecting any one at that particular time and not the least from BODYGUARD since we had moved out, two months earlier to the Tral valley. Our movement was therefore not expected at all. The route was deliberately taken to seek an encounter with the terrorists besides reminding the owners of Rishi carpets to hasten our pending work. Short of Hasan Pur Tabela we were to drive through Turk Tashlu the same village where our brave Nek Singh was injured six months earlier.

As soon as the QRT entered Turk Tashlu, there was visibly a lot of undue activity and running around of people. We quickly realized that something was amiss and probably some terrorists were present in the village. The QRT quickly stopped, jumped out of the vehicles, divided in to three small parties, surrounded and stopped all movement in and outside the village. One individual who tried to run towards north of the village in the direction of the national highway was warned to stop which he didn't. Warning shots were immediately fired. The individual took up a position and took out an AK rifle from underneath his phiren and fired back. Having seen his location, Major Mahesh Thapa who was accompanying the CO, was ordered to surround the terrorist before closing on to him. While the CO covered him from the southern direction Maj Mahesh Thapa quickly surrounded him from the opposite direction.

Troops were warned not to hurry since there was no problem of time: we had to only ensure that there were no casualties to our troops. Attempts to seek his surrender did not yield any result. He was adamant to fight on. In a brief but fierce encounter the terrorist was neutralised. We recovered one AK rifle with three magazines and 61 rounds.

The operation over, we loaded the mortal remains of the terrorist, counted our boys and continued our journey to Hasanpur Tabela. The villagers there confirmed to us that the slain terrorist was a battalion commander of Hizbul Mujahideen responsible for planting IED's on the national highway north and south of Biz Bihara. He had also laid IED's against our unit and against the CO in particular but unfortunately the Gods were not with him. We moved back to our area of Tral where a FIR was lodged with the police and a list of recoveries made was shown to them. The incident was widely reported in the press the next day, commenting on the neat and clean operation. While the terrorist was indeed neutralised there was no collateral damage to either life or property of any villager.

On 8 April we carried out yet another operation in Tral which resulted in the recovery of two weapons. We were provided intelligence input regarding the presence of two to three terrorists in a small village north of Naristan at the end of the Tral valley. The operation was carried out by CO QRT, Maj Sandeep Datta and his Charlie Company. We walked the whole night and managed to surprise the militants who were apprehended without resistance: fortunately they were not armed. Their weapons were tucked away in a hideout near Tral. We walked back the complete distance and brought the militants to Tral. Enroute we recovered the weapons. The GOC 8 Mountain Division Maj Gen (later Lt Gen) D B Shaketkar, VSM who had recently taken over his appointment, visited the unit and had lunch with us in Tral on the same day. He was extremely appreciative of the performance and contribution of the unit. This was reflected in his Demi Official letter that he wrote to us a month later. This is reproduced below.

Major General DB Shekatkar, VSM
General officer Commanding

Headquarters
8 Mountain Division
C/o 56 APO

1564/12/A3

5 May 1995

My Dear Soneja,

1. I take this opportunity to place on record our appreciation and gratitude to you and your Battalion for excellent performance while serving under 8 Mountain Division in most challenging environment.

2. I must honestly state that you all made valuable contribution in bringing down the level of militancy in the valley. There is an appreciable change in general environment. This would not have been possible but for your dedication and sacrifices. 8 Mountain Division can never forget the facts and shall always remain grateful to you all.

3. I take this opportunity to wish you and all ranks of the Battalion a very happy and peaceful tenure at the Peace Station which you all so richly deserve.

With warm regards,

Sd/-x-x-x-x

Col AC Soneja, VSM
CO
2 JAK RIF
C/o 56 APO

Around this period 23 PUNJAB the famous Longewala battalion had been inducted into our area of responsibility. They had just finished their assignment of making of 'BORDER' movie before being inducted into the Valley. They underwent four weeks of training which was followed by a number of joint operations before we finally moved out of the valley on 23April 1995.

In our last operation conducted jointly with 23 PUNJAB on 13 April 1995 Captain Hardeep Singh, SM and L/NK Rajmohan suffered gun shot wounds while operating in the mountainous region of Naristhan. This was ten days before our departure from the valley. The operation resulted in the elimination of three terrorists and recovery of three AK rifles. The operation was led by Lt Col GS Katoch, Maj S K Datta, Maj Mahesh Thapa, Captain Lakhbinder Singh, SM and Captain Hardeep Singh, SM. Captain Amit Chatterjee, our RMO provided immediate aid to Hardeep before he was evacuated to 92 BH. Though he suffered a gun shot wound in his lungs however, he is hail and hearty today and continuing to serve the Indian Army. Lance /Naik Rajmohan also rejoined the unit after a few days in the hospital. Captain Hardeep was awarded a Shaurya Chakra and Rajmohan a commendation card for this operation. As a parting gift the COAS aptly sent us the following message:

Anti terrorist ops by 2 JAK RIF and 23 PUNJAB at NARISTAN MT 9708 on April 13 (.) personal from COAS to CO and all ranks (.) my heartiest congratulations for an excellent ops (.) well done (.) I wish the bns every success in future

---

Ten days later the battalion moved out of the valley on completion of its three year tenure. As we stepped across the Banihal tunnel it gave tremendous satisfaction to all of us for our small but positive contribution in bringing peace to the troubled valley. The battalion left the confines of the beautiful valley taking pride in the fact that there were 358 terrorists less which included 168 killed in 58 successful armed encounters. The battalion carried out a total of 581 operations of which 192 were successful. A recovery of 247 weapons besides a large quantity of ammunition and explosives and warlike stores was a reasonably good effort. One supreme commander, three district commanders and four battalion commanders of various tanjims were neutralised by the unit. A total of 86 awards were earned by the Battalion in its three year tenure in the Valley. We also received 44 complimentary messages which included eight from COAS, nine from GOC-in-C Northern Command and eight from GOC 15 Corps. The unit had received two unit citations and a silver plaque for outstanding performance in J&K from His Excellency The Governor of J&K. We thanked Durge Mata for her blessings and benevolence.

We paid homage to Sub Omkar Singh Manhas and seven other brave soldiers who made the supreme sacrifice in service to the nation. Besides, eight officers five JCOs and 38 OR have left a permanent mark in valley with their blood, resulting from various encounters and IED attacks. Fortunately they were all safe and moved out with the unit.

On 15 August 1995 on the eve of Independence Day late Lance/ Havildar Nek Singh SC was awarded Kirti Chakra for his gallant action that he fought in August 1994. There were four more awards which included three Sena Medals and a commendation card from GOC-in-C. This was followed by 28 **more awards** which were announced on the eve of Army Day and Republic Day 1996. These included one Shaurya Chakra, six Sena Medals, seven commendation cards from COAS, and fourteen from GOC-in-C Northern Command. This was an outstanding recognition of bravery and dedication displayed by the unit. A list of awardees is separately attached. In a rare gesture GOC 15 Corps Lt Gen J S Dhillon sent us a special letter of congratulations and greetings for having been blessed with such a large number of gallantry awards. This letter from the GOC 15 Corps is attached as an appendix.

A few more letters written by senior officers, colleagues and well wishers who constantly blessed us, are also attached as appendices. We received a very large number of letters practically from every senior officer of the regiment, commanding officers and from formation commanders. While it is not possible to attach all these letters we are only attaching about a dozen of them. Many of these senior officers who blessed us have already gone but their blessings continue to be with all ranks of the battalion. They truly reflect the performance and the standing of the unit in Northern Command during that period. We are certain that with the blessings of "Durge Mata" our BODYGURARD Battalion will continue to perform exceedingly well in all operations, training and on issues of man management.

RECEPTION AT ARMY HOUSE 15 JANUARY 1995

With Chief of Army Staff

CHAPTER 5

Case Studies

OP Waltiyang (Waltingu), 5 MAY 1993

This is a story of a daylight, lightning raid carried out by the unit, launched 45 km from our base, in the high mountains of beautiful Kashmir valley, resulting in elimination of Alamdir Kashmir Platoon of Usman Ganai company of Hizbul Mujahideen."

In the summer of 1993, the battalion was deployed in the general area of Prisal, Mamman and Chitargram which are part of Shupian and Kulgam tehsils about 8 km south west of Bij Bihara in the heartland of militancy controlled by the diehard Jammiaties. We moved into this area on 3 March 1993 across the Ram Bihara River which had been quickly bridged by the Division Engineer Regt a few days earlier. Our area formed part of the 'Golden Triangle' of militancy as the civil officials preferred to call it. The triangle was formed by Zainapura, Prisal and Arwani. These three villages alone counted for almost 50 terrorists. There were many more in the villages around, ready to strike and ambush us at every opportunity.

Our area of responsibility lay between the Ram Bihara and Vishwa rivers, where in besides us, we also had the famous 22 GRENADIERS battalion which was deployed towards the south in general area around Shupian-Imam Sahib. Our main task was to restore law and order and to eliminate terrorism in the area. This involved continuous operations against the terrorists in well over 170 villages by day and night. While the terrorists tried to demoralize the security forces by continuous ambushes, laying of improvised explosive devices (IEDs) and firing on the camps, we decided to effectively retaliate, but within the constraints of Human Rights and Do's and Don't's issued by the then Chief Of Army Staff (COAS).

Planning of most operations was based either on specific information or on simple appreciation. One such operation was planned in village Bolus of Kulgam tehsil in South Kashmir. We received information of presence of a group of terrorists in the village. This was about 8 kms from Prisal. We planned to carry out a first light cordon and search operation for which we left our location at 0200 h on 5 May 1993 on foot so that we could surprise the terrorists. The village was approached from four directions as shown in the sketch. The cordon was effective by 0430 h and after the break of dawn we asked for all men to come out and assemble at the crossroads. A quick three hour search revealed us a water bottle cover only.

There was no trace of terrorists whatsoever, or even if there were, we could not find one. It took us 19 more months to eliminate terrorists of this village on New Year Day of January 95 after a 28 hour long encounter. That's a different story and will be discussed later in the script.

When the three hour search did not reveal anything worthwhile we decided to do something afresh. Our brave second in command Major Harbans along with our efficient adjutant Lakhi who was always full of life, suggested that we send out two 'seek encounter patrols of one officer and six other ranks each. We quickly made a plan and requisitioned two vehicles, a taxi and a bus. The patrols were to be led by the second in command and by the adjutant. Incidentally the same adjutant, three days earlier in a similar operation in taxi had surprised a militant near village Nilou in Kulgam tehsil. The militant was merrily walking along the road with an AK rifle slung on his right shoulder. When challenged to stop he opened fire, he was neutralized in a brief firefight.

After a quick breakfast of aloo-parathas, which was the favourite of young officers, the patrols started towards their respective destinations. Harbans, being senior, besides having been tasked to cover a longer distance was given the taxi and Lakhi the civil bus. At 0900 h the patrol led by the adjutant saw two suspicious looking men moving along the road. The vehicle was quickly stopped, troops dismounted and challenged the duo.

They were wearing blue sports shoes and both sported long beards. On being challenged they took to their heels. The brave adjutant and Lance/ Naik Nek Singh immediately chased them. After a brief scuffle both were caught. They were not fired upon since they were unarmed.

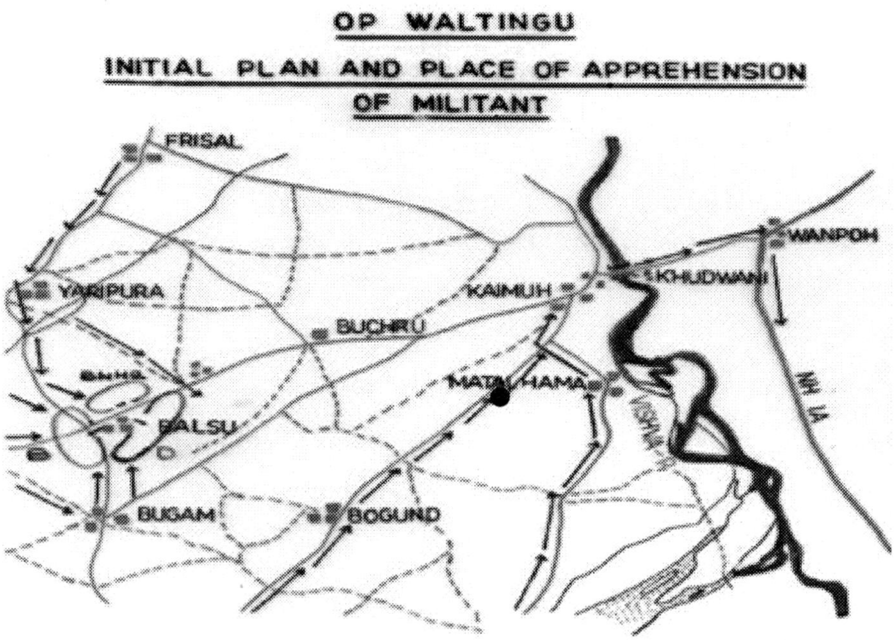

Place of Apprehension ●

Operation Waltingu: Initial Plan and Place of Apprehension of Militant

A quick 'on the spot investigation' by Lakhbinder revealed that both were Pakistan trained terrorists of Hizbul Mujahedeen based at a hideout located 45 km away. They belonged to Alamdir Kashmir Platoon of Usman Ganai Company. One of them was a section commander and the other a ranker. The latter had come to his house in village Bugam on short leave. Since he did not return in time and had become 'Absent without leave' the section commander was sent to apprehend him. They were both returning to their camp near Waltiyang which is located 45 Km away, about 10 Kms south of Qazikund.

Lakhi quickly informed the commanding officer who instructed Harbans to immediately join up with the adjutant and carryout further interrogation. He had by then become an expert at interrogation of terrorists. Meanwhile at Bolus the commanding officer got hold of another civil bus, ordered the CO QRT (Quick Reaction Team) with 2/Lt Hardeep as our intelligence officer to board the bus. 2/Lt Ashish Maini officiating company commander, who was by chance standing close by, requested for permission to accompany the patrol, which was immediately granted. He joined up with one junior commissioned officer and two other ranks. Major GS Katoch the unit third senior most officer was ordered to take over the search that was continuing at Bolus while the commanding officer with the QRT linked up with Lakhi.

On link up, the terrorists were further interrogated. Thereafter a quick plan was made. The brigade commander was informed and requested for permission to carry out a day light raid on the militant hideout. Brigadier A S Khanna, VrC in turn asked the General Officer Commanding since we were to move through the area of responsibility of two different formations. The permission was quickly granted and we commenced our move towards Kaimuh where we had to cross the Vishwa River over a boat bridge. Our raiding party comprised of five officers, two junior commissioned officers and 34 other ranks in two taxis and a bus.

As the patrol moved, news of the apprehension of militants spread like wildfire. Messages were quickly passed by the militants. We intercepted a message by one station telling the other that we were travelling in civil pattern vehicles. This was confirmed to us by our brigade staff later but people did not expect us to raid a 2500M high mountainous hideout located 45 km away absolutely far away from our area of responsibility. The militants also did not know that the unit had some of the most magnificent officers, JCOs and men on the orbat who could produce wonderful results.

We arrived at Kaimuh, paid the drivers, ran across the boat bridge, quickly grabbed two matadors and started off for our objective. At Bunigam near km 229 on NH1A we turned due south, drove across the Vishwa river since the water level was low, pushing the vehicles literally when we got stuck and finally arrived at Waltiyang. In between we got stuck at Naubug once again. Fortunately for the battalion the water level being low we could negotiate, later we realized that the water level generally rises in the afternoon hours due to melting of snow with the rising sun. The patrols arrived at the pictures-que destination on the foothills of Pir Panjal at about 1230 h. Standing close to the historical Zairat under the wings of the Pir

Baba, the area looked peaceful and majestic. The peaks were covered with snow. It was a remarkable place indeed.

Before entering the village we left one stop consisting of one NCO and four other ranks north of the village and another stop of four other ranks towards the southern end of the village near the famous Zairat. While we sought the blessing of God Almighty before commencing our move up the difficult hills, the stops kept a check on the population and also ensured that our transport did not run away leaving us high and dry in the wilderness. By mistake we left Lance/Naik Shamsher at the first stop, he was the one carrying our maps and thereafter when the staff at the brigade asked us about our area we could only give them our approximate location. We realized our mistake, however on that day the commander did manage to reach us a few hours later.

At 1300 h the raiding party divided itself into three patrols on the advice of one of the terrorists who was accompanying us. He happened to be the section commander whom we had apprehended a few hours earlier in the day. It was this man, the section commander who suggested to us that a small group should directly approach the hideout while the other two patrols should cover the northern and the southern flanks. As events unfolded his advice proved quite useful. Captain Lakhbinder Singh and 2/ Lt Ashish Maini with a patrol of 7 ORs were tasked to silence the sentries, while one JCO and 9 ORs with IO as part of the CO QRT, and Maj Harbans with one JCO and 9 OR moved from either flank to raid the hideout. Of the two militants that had been apprehended, the section commander was with the Adjutant while the other boy was detailed to accompany Harbans.

The sentry silencing patrol under the adjutant moved along a spur on a 70 degree slope making effective use of cover. It was a difficult move indeed. The section commander also helped them move along the correct route. Enroute they met a group of Gujjars with whom the patrol had an interesting conversation. The sentry silencing patrol incidentally was dressed like the terrorists. Lance/Naik Nek Singh who was in the lead spoke in perfect Kashmiri telling the Gujjars that they were mujahids returning after ambushing an army patrol. They had captured a Radio Set and were now looking for their brethren. The gujjars advised them to continue up the slope on the same route and that they would meet the terrorists soon.

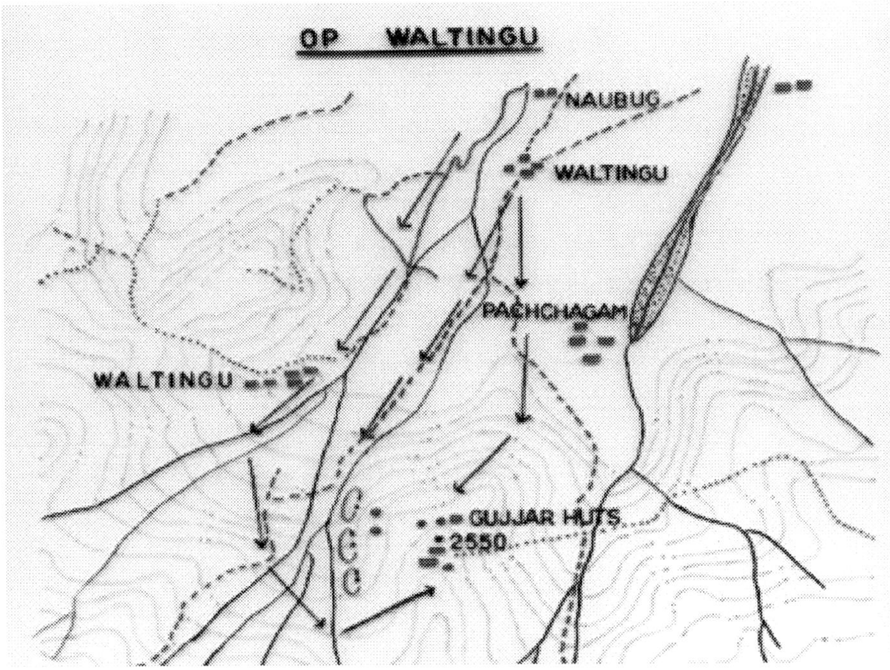

Day Light Raid at Militant Hideout

At 1430 h the patrol under the adjutant reached about 100 m short of the objective. They could see two Gujjar huts and on one of them they saw a terrorist leisurely sitting. Captain Lakhbinder Singh alongwith Lance/ Naik Nek Singh crawled towards one of the gujjar huts, where as 2/Lt Ashish Mani alongwith Naik Pawan Kumar established a stop with an aim to intercept terrorists who would try to escape. The Adjutant and Lance/Naik Nek Singh entered the hut where they had seen the terrorist. They also now saw four more sitting on top of the next hut barely 20 meters away, with weapons in their hands. The terrorist in the first hut was completely surprised and neutralized on the spot. One AK 56 rifle was recovered from him. The remaining terrorists now opened up a volley of fire. In a daring action Lakhi with his buddy charged at the next hut and killed one more terrorist from whom another AK 56 rifle was recovered. Taken aback the terrorists attempted to escape and ran in different directions. One of them ran in the direction of 2/Lt Maini and Naik Pawan Kumar. He was soon neutralized and his rifle recovered.

Two terrorists slid down the hill side and were soon spotted with their weapons shining by the CO, almost from a km away. The CO alongwith Hardeep and the rest of the patrol ran and closed the escape route. This was the fastest run the CO (a cross country runner in his younger days) had run in his life. Even Hardeep complained that he was left far behind. It wasn't a competition; the route of the terrorists had to be blocked, it was a case of life and death for the terrorists and of course prestige for the BODYGUARDs. The terrorists finding themselves blocked took up positions and started firing at our boys. Harbans too was asked to close in and the terrorists were soon completely surrounded. They were advised and ordered to surrender, however, they continued to fire. Rifleman Naresh Kumar and his buddy both part of the CO's patrol in a daring action charged at the bush in which they were hiding and killed both of them. Rifleman Naresh received gun shot wounds on his left hand and shoulder. Two AK 56 rifles were recovered from the terrorists.

During the subsequent search of the huts occupied by the terrorists by the adjutant one more AK 56 rifle was recovered. The hideout was later destroyed. A total of six AK 56 rifles with 16 Magazines, 440 live rounds and three grenades were recovered. All the terrorists killed were from Aalamdir Kashmir platoon of Usman Ganai company. Meanwhile, of the two terrorists who had acted as our guides, the section commander seized an opportunity during the fire fight and managed to escape. He unfortunately had to pay a very heavy price for that. The other boy returned with us to the camp and was handed over to the police.

A little later the Brigade Commander Brig A S Khanna, VrC along with his Deputy Commander, the brigade DQ and OC ADS reached Waltiyang and complimented the boys for a very successful raid. Our commander had just returned from leave a day before and was visibly happy to see the operation having been conducted so smoothly. The success of the operation was commended by GOC-in-C Northern Command and also by other senior commanders. The brigade in its monthly report to Division Headquarters recorded that "it was a lightning raid conducted by the unit".

The return journey was equally interesting. We started from Waltiyang at about 1900 h. The dependable matadors this time got stuck in a nala near Naubug less than a km from Waltiyang because of increase of water level in the rivers. Fortunately once again we found a bus on the other side of the river to help us return. There was a quick search all around and we got hold of the bus driver. All stores were quickly shifted; we cleared our bills with the drivers of matadors and recommenced our journey. Short of NH1A near Bunigam, the bus driver refused to enter Vishwa River and so we got down and walked through the river and came up to NH1A. After sometime we saw a truck coming from Srinagar and heading towards Qazigund. It was quickly stopped; since it was empty we turned it back. We rode all the way for the next 25 km through Khanabal, Bij Bihara and on to Arwani. All through the journey we kept our fingers crossed fearing an attack at any moment. We crossed the Vishwa river again, this time with help of ferries, walked through Arwani and boarded our transport outside the village. We finally returned to our camp in Prisal at 2300 h, exactly 21 hours after leaving the camp.

The operation did not end there on that day. Early next morning the family of the section commander who had escaped while climbing up to the hide out a day before, arrived at our camp in Prisal. We told his family and people of his village that he indeed was the person who took us to the hideout. All our success was because of him, we were in fact grateful to him for his assistance. He had now run away and would be caught by the militants. We asked the parents to motivate their ward to surrender to us, which they did not. Three days later on 9 May he was caught and executed by his colleagues. We learnt later that the terrorists led by one code captain (self styled) Firoz had cut his calf muscles and handed them to him. And half an hour later the section commander was shot dead. As luck would have it, the ring leader captain Firoz of village Kunzar who had done this execution was himself killed, once again by our taxiborne patrol led by our young officers within one hour of that unfortunate inhuman execution by the terrorists.

The operation brought us appreciation from various quarters. There was a good coverage in the local press. Both the print media and the newly formed electronic media like the Zee News etc. covered it well. The formation commanders had already sent us their appreciation. We thanked Durge Mata and the God Almighty for their help and blessings and closed the operation the next day with a bottle of champagne and a Barakhana (a community meal) for the troops.

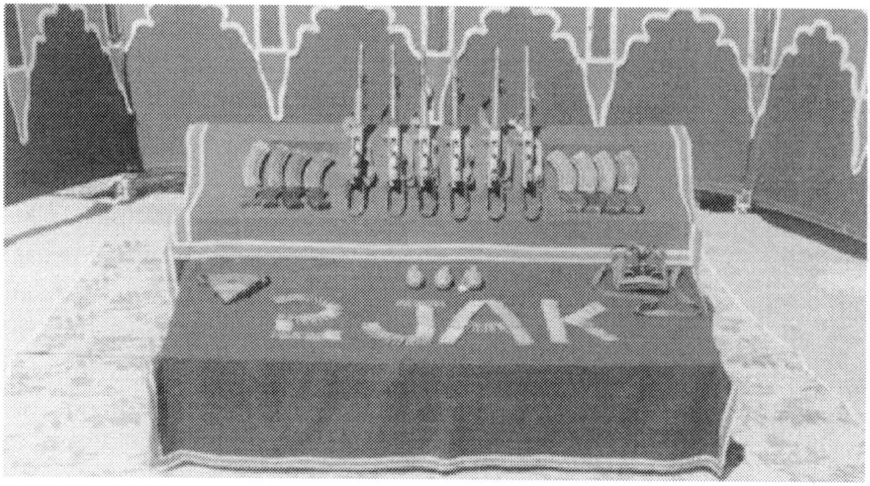

Recoveries OP Waltiyung, 5 May 1993

THE TURKPURA ENCOUNTER

This is a story of another day light encounter conducted by our unit in the semi mountainous region around village Turkpura of Bandipur Tehsil which lies on the foothills along the Northern banks of Wuler Lake. This village is located along the Northern loop of Road Bandipur–Malangam–Sopur. Between Bandipur and Malangam – the road divides itself in two loops. While the Southern loop skirts the Wuler Lake, the Northern one goes along the foothills. This is about 7 kms stretch. Half way through is the famous Putushai feature which overlooks a village called Manangnipura. This entire area including the Putushai feature has, over the years, seen a large number of bullets flying, numerous encounters and ambushes. Every convoy of the security forces was fired upon from this very feature particularly on its return journey if not secured by troops in time.

The terrorists of the area often took up good firing positions on this feature and engaged convoys of security forces. When chased, they would run northwards, climb on to Turkpura feature and continue up towards Hampathri and then to the ridge line. It was extremely difficult to chase terrorists uphill and most troops normally gave it up half way through. The terrorists therefore felt quite confident and safe to operate in this area. They also knew the routine and pattern of movement of security forces.

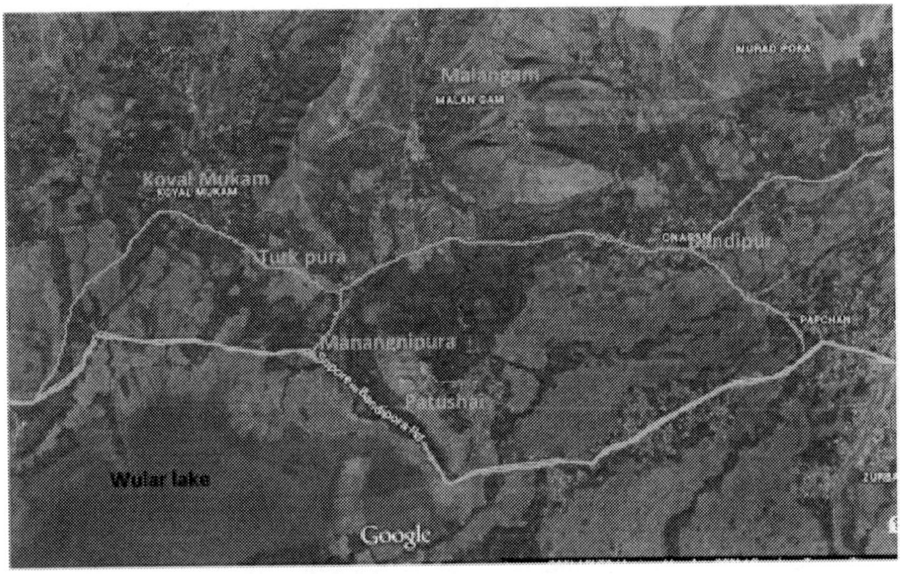

Area of Operations—Turkpura

Our battalion arrived in this sector from South Kashmir on 10 Jul 1993 in high spirits. The previous week in our old location at Prisal-Yaripura had been extremely violent. We had recovered five AK Rifles, killed two and apprehended three terrorists. This however, was at a considerable price. Two of our officers, i.e., the second in command and the quartermaster had been injured and evacuated to 92 Base Hospital in Srinagar. Fortunately they recovered very soon. Immediately after arrival in this sector, we were involved in yet another operation on 15 July 1993 in which we had neutralized 8 terrorists including the Deputy Commander in Chief of Hizbul Mujahideen Wafadar Khan. On the same day a patrol under Subedar Adjutant Faiju Ram while conveying a wounded soldier to Bandipur was fired upon from the same Putushai feature which has been discussed earlier. The alert JCO immediately retaliated and chased the miscreants till Turkpura where they killed one terrorist.

Five days later, on 20 Jul 1993 we decided to carryout reconnaissance and area domination of Sonawari Tehsil. This was supposed to be an easy operation being undertaken primarily to, not to over involve ourselves on that day. The Commander was on leave and we thought we could relax after a short operation. The target area lay generally to the South West of Safapura and Manasbal lake. The rifle companies at Bandipur and Safapura had been tasked to secure road Manasbal-Bandipur and to provide a safe corridor to the convoys leading to Sangerwain which was the base for troops deployed along the line of control in that sector. 20 July was the convoy day which meant that two companies would have to be left for securing the road axis. These two companies left for their assigned tasks at about 0800 h. Therefore only two rifle companies were available for operation that day.

About two and half hours later i.e., around 1030 h while the CO was leaving for a similar task with his QRT, Maj (later Brig) AP Tripathi the Brigade Major came running and intercepted the CO near the exit gate of the brigade. He told us that he had received specific information about presence of some terrorists in village Turkpura which was 30 Km away and 'whether we would like to take action on it. "Most certainly" the CO assured him and quickly calling for the map carried out a brief appreciation, prepared his plan, discussed it with officiating adjutant 2/Lt Hardeep Singh affectionately called 'Hardy' and his Intelligence Officer (IO) 2/Lt Ashish Maini. The plan was taken to the Brigade Commander who approved the same immediately.

Plan

The administrative convoy for Kanzalwan sector was to pass through Safapura at about 1300 h. By about 1500 h the road securing companies used to return to the respective camps. To achieve surprise we decided to move at the tail of the returning convoy to Bandipur and show to the public that it was only a routine movement. We decided to raid Turkpura simultaneously rushing in form north east, east, south east and from southern directions. The commander was to follow us too. The raid was to be carried out at 1630 h that day.

Both rifle companies which had gone out for area domination were recalled, given quick lunch and ordered to prepare for the impending task. Officiating company commander of 'D' Company at Bandipur 2Lt Tripathi was briefed on the move. We adjusted our speed so as to coordinate the simultaneous arrival at the objective by troops of D and B companies. Hardy my Adjutant was tasked to lead 'B' Company moving on the heals of platoon of Delta Company under 2/Lt Tripathi.

Conduct

Moving out at about 1430 h we managed to achieve total surprise. Once near the objective, officers were told that there would be no halts, no confirmatory briefing and no wastage of time. As brought out earlier 2/Lt Tripathi was briefed on the move itself. Our technique of raiding a village during day time included a rush into the village from different directions, freezing all movements followed by, a thorough search of the complete village. Normally the CO QRT and one company used to rush inside while the others ran around and covered all exits of the village. The drills were quite well rehearsed and taped up. On arrival at about 1600 h, Hardy was to rush along the Eastern flank climb on to the spur and continue climbing on to Point 2283 which overlooks vill Turkpura from north and east. It was a difficult climb, not of his choice; nevertheless he did the job remarkably well.

Just as we entered the village a group of terrorists ran out of it, into north eastern direction towards Point 2283. Terrorists took up positions behind boulders in the Nala and that was the mistake they made. We quickly surrounded them. Notwithstanding his exuberance Hardy was ordered not to charge at the terrorists till we surrounded them completely. The terrorists were ordered to surrender but they refused to listen and continued firing at our boys. The firefight lasted for a little over 15 minutes. One of the terrorists in an attempt to throw a grenade at us blasted himself accidentally thereby further reducing the fire fight. Our brigade commander by then had arrived at the objective and had taken up a vantage position at Pt 1964 immediately west of the village. He was witness to the gallantry displayed by the unit personnel and complimented all those who had participated in this brave action.

The operation resulted in elimination of five terrorists and apprehension of another two. A total of two AK rifles, two pistols and 184 rounds of ammunition were recovered. The dead militants included, a dreaded Regimental commander of Hizbullah Tanjim code Capt Dilawar who was on the run for a long time. We also received a number of complimentry messages from the Brigade, Division and the Corps commanders.

The Kondabal Operation
27 & 28 September 1993

Ever since we shifted to the area of Safapura, we were regularly fired upon by terrorists from across the Manasbal lake either from the high feature of Ahteng or from the area of Kondabal. The usual routine was, that all lights would be switched off immediately and troops would retaliate from their pre prepared positions. The fire from both sides was rarely effective due to long ranges. We very soon changed this practice and decided to go out as soon as we were fired upon. We decided to try and surround them. The message was immediately conveyed and the instances of firing reduced considerably thereafter.

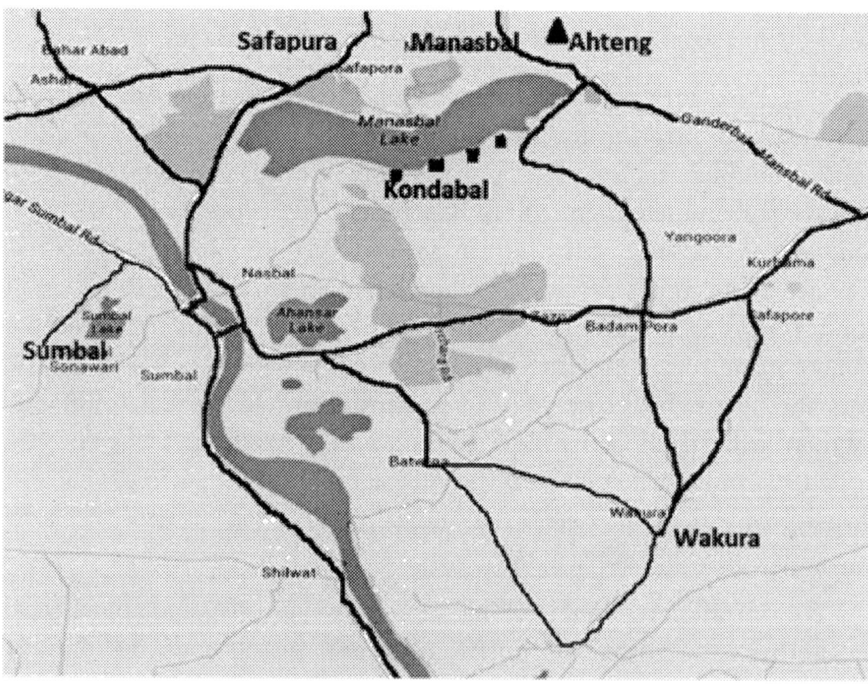

Area of Operations Symbal-Safapura-Wakura

We changed the timings of our operations too. Once we went early morning for a cordon and search operation, returned at about the midday, broke off and then reassembled again after half an our and relaunched ourselves for yet another operation. Change of tactics did not always bring in success but it kept the terrorists on their toes.

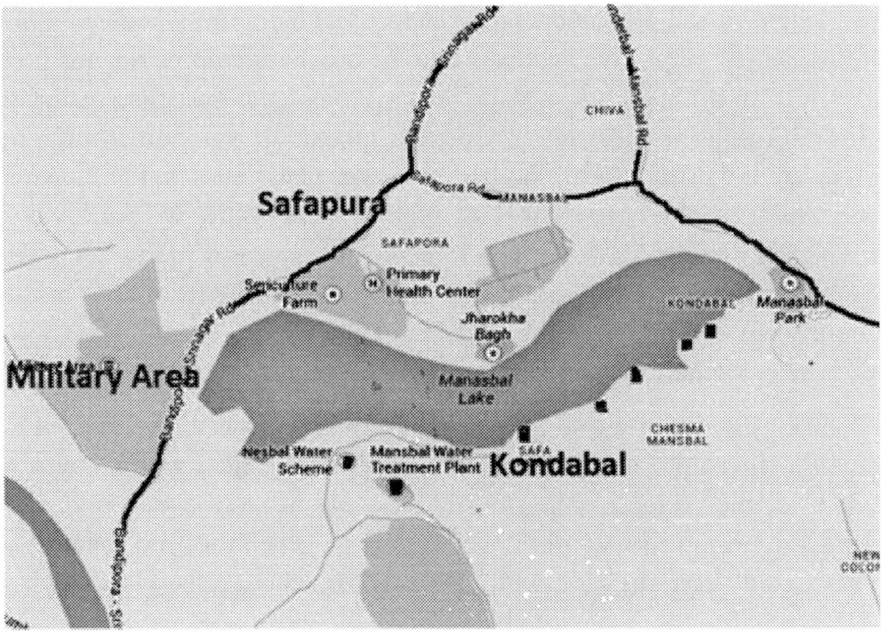

Operation Kondabal

It was one such day in end of September 1993 that we decided to strike at Kondabal in the afternoon. We made a two sided approach and quickly surrounded the village, got the men together and carried out a quick search of the entire village. This village was spread along the southern bank of Manasbal Lake in a linear fashion. There were a number of terrorists from this village. One of them was known to have thrown a handgrenade at his father who was more than twice his size. Whenever we came to this village, while rest of the villagers sat on the ground this man was forced to sit on a chair, in order to give him due respect because of his stature and age. The complete village had seen that. We were told by the village head (also called maqdam), that all terrorists of the village had disappeared and were missing for many months. The Maqdam's son was a terrorist too and every one told us the often repeated story that their particular wards had not been seen for many months.

On that particular day we were in a hurry too, next morning the new General Officer Commanding Major General SS Grewal, SM, VSM was to visit the formation headquarters. In order to prepare for the next day we decided to call off the operation before last light and asked every one to board their respective vehicles. One of our boys who could not hold himself from the call of the nature, decided to enter a lime stone quarry to relieve himself. Soon as he entered the quarry, he saw something and immediately ran out. What he had seen was a mat and freshly prepared food which clearly meant that someone was there inside. We quickly sent in a search party alongwith a few torches. The cave was pretty long. The search party kept moving inside and suddenly drew fire from deep inside. There were at least two weapons that opened up, so our fears were confirmed, we had the terrorists trapped inside the lime stone quarry.

Troops were ordered to immediately debus from their vehicles and re-establish the cordon of the village. However the villagers were allowed to stay inside their respective houses and were told not to move around. One of the first things that we decided was to get a generator from the unit so that we could keep the cave (which actually turned out to be a long tunnel) well lit up at night. We were able to push the terrorists quite deep inside the cave, where we were able to block their movements. Firing was not effective. We fired a couple of smoke grenades and came out of the cave. The cave was well guarded, we searched the area all around to ensure that there was no other opening or exit available. There was none. Having assured ourselves that the terrorists could not escape, we left one company to guard and protect and rest of the boys returned to the unit lines at Safapura. Next morning we continued with the operation.

The visit of Major General SS Grewal, SM, VSM General Officer Commanding started at the appropriate time. The moment he came to the Brigade Headquarters he asked us the reason for not finishing the operation in time on the previous evening. We told him that there was no hurry and that the time was with us, we assured him that we would get them very soon. The staff at the Brigade and Divisional Headquarters had picked up wireless information of some important terrorists trapped inside a cave in Kondabal. Towards mid day we fired a couple of smoke bombs alongwith a few tear gas shells that had been borrowed from the police. The combined effect of the two was disastrous for the terrorists inside the cave. Soon thereafter three militants ran out firing their weapons and tried to break the cordon. Since the cave was well covered the terrorists could not escape and in exchange of fire all three of them were neutralized and their weapons recovered.

One of the terrorist turned out to be a company commander and the other two platoon commanders. The missing son of the village head was unfortunately also there. It was a good catch. Durge Mata was kind; there were no casualties to our troops in this operation. This success was complimented upon both by the General Officers Commanding 15 Corps and 8 Mountain Division.

OPERATION ALPINE NOOSE

Operation Alpine Noose is a story of a murderous operation carried out by 81 Mountain Brigade and attached troops on the famous heights of Malangam bowl on 6 Oct 1993. The operation resulted in killing of 23 terrorists including six Afghan and one Pakistani national and apprehension of one. Needless to add there was a recovery of a large number of sophisticated weapons, ammunition and explosives. There were 99 detonators too, besides others, which resulted in elimination of 99 improvised explosive devices which the terrorists could have made.

Malangam bowl lies along the northern banks of famous Wular lake, the biggest fresh water lake in Asia, in Bandipur Tehsil of Baramula district. The bowl lies along infiltration routes of terrorists coming in from Pakistan Occupied Kashmir via Lolab valley that lies due west and North West and second from Gurez Sector. Terrorists were known to be regularly using these routes to move to other parts of the valley. Due to shortage of troops and the lay of ground, which gave them good observation and domination, the terrorists by and large, could easily escape the dragnet of security forces. In July 1993, 10 BIHAR and later 2 JAK RIF achieved spectacular successes eliminating almost 20 terrorists in one month including the deputy commander in Chief and district commander of Hizbul Mujahideen in North Kashmir, on 15 Jul 1993. By September–October that year, the situation in this area had again gone bad and terrorists were reported to be moving about quite freely on the upper reaches of hills dominating the Malangam bowl and the Wular lake.

On 2 Oct 1993, the day of Mahatma Gandhi Jyanti the battalion operations groups of the Brigade alongwith Col TS Hassanwalia the officiating brigade commander carried out a reconnaissance of Sopur, the hot bed of militancy and terrorism. 11 RAJ RIF which was then located in Bandipur, provided us secure passage while moving along Bandipur–Sopur road. On our return from Sopur that afternoon the militants once again were able to fire on the road opening patrol, near Malangam. The fire caused us one casualty; a boy from 11 RAJ RIF was injured and evacuated to Bandipur. Terrorists raised anti national slogans from top of the ridges. In a calculated move the officiating commander decided not to retaliate since we were neither prepared, nor had adequate strength for chasing the terrorists uphill during day which would have certainly brought us none or little dividends. Back in Bandipur we heard terrorists raising slogans over the captured radio sets. The country had suffered a massive earthquake in Latur (in Maharashtra) four days earlier. The militants prayed the rest of country a similar fate. It was quite demoralizing, Col TS Hassanwalia advised restrain and assured us that we will return very soon, fully prepared and then take them on. We all agreed and returned to Safapura by evening.

True to his word Col TS Hassanwalia visited the Division Headquarters the next day and got the necessary sanction for launching a large size cordon and search operation in the area of Malangam after three days. The General Officer Commanding, Maj Gen SS Grewal, SM, VSM provided additional resources besides of course his blessings. The additional resources allotted to the Brigade for this operation were:

(a) 2 SIKH less a Company ex 56 Infantry Brigade.
(b) Team ex 9 PARA
(c) One company ex 10 BIHAR of 192 Infantry Brigade.
(d) Two companies from 13 KUMAON ex 268 Infantry Brigade.

Operation was planned to be carried out in three phases which included:

(a) To establish a cordon of general area Malangam with four battalions and simultaneously establish deep stops by 10 BIHAR, 9 PARA and 13 KUMAON.
(b) Carry out a sweep of the ridge line and all hills descending to the Malangam bowl.
(c) Carry out a thorough search of the densely populated area of Malangam bowl.

Area of Operations Kupwara-Bandipur-Wular Lake

D Day (Day of operation) selected was 6 October 1993. We wargamed our plans in the Brigade Headquarters on the 4 October and tied up various loose ends between all the units participating in the operation.

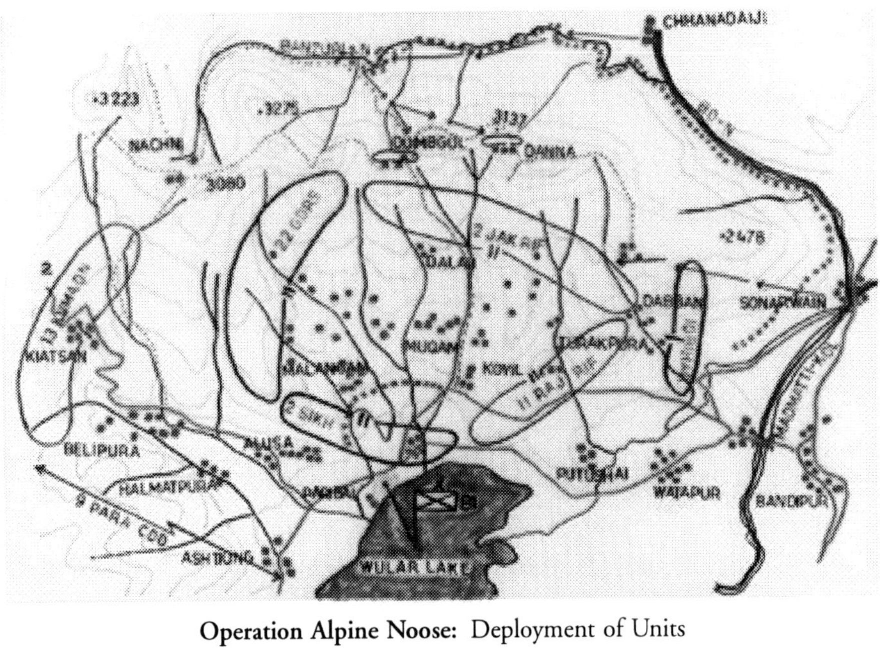

Operation Alpine Noose: Deployment of Units

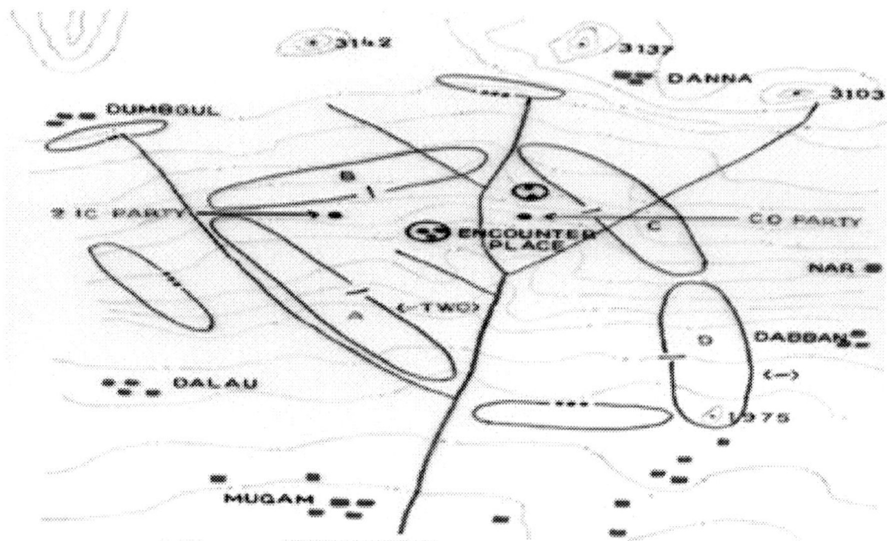

Operation Alpine Noose: Deployment of BODYGUARD Bn, 6 October 1993

Execution

The Operation started on 5 October with 22 GRENADIERS leaving their location at Sumbal near Safapura for Kupwara so as to approach the objective over the hill feature via the Naachna Pass, almost simultaneously we moved up to Sonarwain alongwith the ‘up convoy of formation in Gurez Sector. On arrival in Sonarwain at about 1000 h on 5 October 1993, all ranks were ordered to move in to available shelters as planned. No movement was permitted in and out of the camp so as to avoid suspicion about the impending task. At 2030 h the same evening battalion less two companies with a company of 10 BIHAR moved out of Sonarwain camp, and moving stealthily along upper reaches without disturbing the village guard dogs, the group arrived in the objective area by 0330 h on 6 October 1993. The other two companies under the dynamic and energetic second in command Maj Harbans Gill had earlier moved out in transport at about 1800 h into the opposite direction. They drove on to Tragbal forest along road to Kanjalwan. Having reached Tragbal forest they left their vehicles at Chhandaji and commenced the balance movement on foot. Moving along Banzuri N they climbed to Dumbgul and deployed themselves in general area Dumbgul–Danna by 0530 h on 6 October.

Conduct

All troops having got into their respective positions the sweep operation commenced at 0730 h by all units as planned. One platoon each of A and B Companies which had moved under Major Harbans Gill were asked to continue to be at Dumbgul and Dalau to cover the ridge line. During the night it had rained around 0345h for good over an hour. All company commanders were instructed to ensure that troops got under cover but were not allowed to light any fire. It is to the credit of brave soldiers that they obeyed the orders despite extreme cold and rain. This enabled us to maintain surprise and their movements were not picked up by anyone in the Malangam bowl. Later when the sweep commenced from the direction of Wular lake, by other battalions, one group of terrorists, as was their practice, started climbing up towards Dalau and were planning to escape to Dumbgul and then to the area North of it. They moved right in to the area which was guarded by our boys. The sequence of events thereafter went about as follows:

(a) At about 0810 h a stop of Charlie Company saw two persons moving in a suspicious manner in a Nala about 150 meters down stream. They were challenged and later engaged by fire. A quick search by Maj Rajesh Sood revealed two AK 56 rifles with magazines and ammunition.

(b) Around the same time 2/Lt Hardeep Singh, officiating company commander of 'B' company deployed at Dalau saw about 15 persons who were initially moving up suddenly turned and started running down. He chased them with the personnel of his company headquarters. Only a few of them appeared to be armed. A quick firefight resulted in killing of five terrorists. An immediate search of the area revealed only one AK rifle.

(c) The same group referred above was also seen moving by 2/Lt Vinay Shahi who happened to be deployed with the northern most stop of 'C' Company. Remaining terrorists now took up cover on the feature opposite Vinay about 150 meters away and started intense firing with a variety of weapons including a UMG, and a Rocket launcher.

(d) CO meanwhile moved up with his quick reaction team (QRT) and reinforced 2/Lt Vinay Shahi. About half of the QRT of the original strength of 20 ORs was sent with Harbans the second in command, the previous night along the Tragbal route. Of the remaining 'half' the officiating Adjutant 2/Lt Ashish Maini was sent alongwith five OR to skirt the feature occupied by the terrorists from South and to climb up from their rear. Therefore the CO reinforced Vinay Shahi with remaining five other ranks.

(e) Maj Harbans moving down from Dumbgul was also engaged by terrorists with a GPMG. Ashish Maini was ordered to move up and reinforce Harbans which he immediately did. Harbans and his brave team killed five terrorists and recovered one GPMG that was engaging them.

(f) Maj Rajesh Sood at this stage was ordered to re-deploy one platoon to cover Eastern and North Eastern ridges while Maj Nitin Bhatnagar was ordered to readjust and cover a Nala going down to the Malangam bowl. Maj Ghanshyam Katoch moving west of Harbans patrol was also ordered to quickly linkup with the latter so as to effectively block all escape routes. The terrorists were therefore effectively blocked from all directions.

(g) The whole hill side was reverberating with fire of automatic weapons. To thousands of people who heard the gun fire that day, there appeared to be a war on. Personnel from other units later confirmed to us that there was total pin drop silence in the entire region. Everyone had taken cover and were getting ready for a backlash. All markets were closed, shutters were down, streets were deserted, and buses, taxies and trucks, and almost every thing had come to a grinding halt in the entire area. Most radio sets in the Brigade were tuned to our battalion frequency (this we learnt later), and almost the entire brigade were witness to actions of BODYGUARD battalion. The fire fight continued for nearly eight hours. Repeated attempts to appeal to the terrorists to cease fire had no effect.

(h) 2/Lt Vinay's stop which had been reinforced was maneuvered to close up with the terrorists. Led by our brave force multiplier Havildar Nek Singh and Havildar Shamsher the patrol closed up with the terrorists. Their movement was picked by the terrorists who fired a RPG round which fortunately for us, narrowly missed hitting our boys. We responded with Rocket launcher fire which pinned them down totally. 2/Lt Vinay alongwith Rifleman Sudhir Kumar crawling slowly and stealthily closed up with the terrorists from a flank. The terrorists were hiding behind rocks and bushes. The brave officer personally shot dead three terrorists while Sudhir counted for two more. They recovered two AK rifles in the bargain.

(i) It was 1400 h by then, the fire of terrorists after almost six hours of intense fire fight became sporadic. Since a large number of terrorists were expected to be still hiding, Harbans, assisted by Ghanshyam and Ashish Maini, were asked to sweep the area north to south and west to east along the natural slope of the hills. At about 1500 h Maj Ghanshyam recovered five bodies of terrorists in dense under growth. At that instant one terrorist was heard moving about in the bushes. Ghanshyam surrounded the area and ordered the terrorist to come out and surrender. He did come out but with a grenade in his hand, in the fire fight, before the terrorist could throw his grenade at our troops, he was shot through his stomach with grenade tearing apart in to two. Suddenly another AK rifle opened up from the undergrowth. There were two more terrorists there, who were quickly silenced by the brave boys of Alpha Company under Major Ghanshyam Katoch. In this brief encounter, three terrorists were killed and three weapons recovered including one rocket launcher, one AK 56 rifle and one pistol.

(j) In the final search by personnel of CO QRT and troops of Charlie Company one UMG and a large quantity of ammunition and explosives including 99 electric detonators were also recovered. At this stage one terrorist who was hiding in the bushes was apprehended and handed over to the police.

The fire subsided by about 1700 h which was followed by a through search of the area that revealed a total of 23 terrorists killed in the day long encounter. The operation was duly witnessed by the complete formation, the Police and by large section of villagers in the Malangam bowl. At about last light which was about 1900 h after taking clearance from the officiating commander we returned to our camp at Safapura for a well earned sleep after 36 hours. The first thing on the return was a visit to the unit temple which was our practice to thank the God Almighty and our 'DURGE MATA' who had been extremely kind to us. We suffered no casualties which happened only because of their blessings. That we were fully convinced. We prayed for their continued guidance and benevolence.

The most satisfying part of the operation was that the battalion with the blessing Durge Mata had not suffered any injury to any individual despite over eight hours of intense firefight. Most officers had narrow misses including the commanding officer. All officers were time and again cautioned to be careful and that there should be no unnecessary bravado. All youngsters in particular were told that the Commanding officer would like to see their dresses absolutely soaked in mud which they would get only in case they crawled in face of militant fire. Our young Hardy had the guts to even caution the Commanding Officer to not to close up with the terrorists 'since the bullets were flying' he said on the radio set. He was told to keep quiet and concentrate on his task. The CO meanwhile had joined up with Vinay Shahi and taken position right opposite a group of terrorists who were neutralized with combined efforts of all officers, JCO and our brave boys.

Achievements

(a) *Terrorists Killed/Apprehended*

- (i) killed - 23
- (ii) Apprehended - 01

(b) *Weapons Recovered*

- (i) GPMG - 01
- (ii) UMG - 01
- (iii) RPG 7 V - 01
- (iv) Rif AK 56 - 06
- (v) Pistol 9mm - 01

(c) *Ammunition*

- (i) Small Arms - 569
- (ii) Grenades - 08
- (iii) Mines A/Personnel - 03

(d) *Miscellaneous*

- (i) Radio set (ICON) - 01
- (ii) Electric detonators - 99
- (iii) Fuze wire - 10 meters
- (iv) Binocular - 01
- (v) Bayonet - 01

2nd SIKH while carrying out search in area of Malangam also recovered one pistol. Therefore the operation resulted in recovery of 11 weapons besides a large quantity of ammunition and explosives. It was the biggest encounter fought within the valley till then. Though on the LC there had been bigger successes however in the valley this was the biggest as claimed by DGP J&K in a public statement. It was later revealed that this group had come from Sopur and was tasked to exfiltrate to POK so as to guide a group of 150 terrorists in to Sopur for its defense against an impending operation by the security forces. Therefore the entire group was not armed. They included six Afghan and one POK national whose mortal remains lie buried in the village of Muqam. The elimination of the group did make our task comparatively easier when we went into Sopur seven weeks later. By about 1900 h on 6 October, we were able to hand over the mortal remains of slain terrorists to DSP Bandipur who was dutifully waiting with his patrol there. Two hours later, we were back in our camp at Safapura.

Next morning the GOC 8 Mountain Division, GOC 15 Corps and GOC-in-C Northern Command sent us a complimentry messages which summed up performance of the unit in this operation. Both the Army Chief and the Army Commander specifically complimented all ranks of the unit for an excellent operation.

OP Alpine Noose, 6 October 1993

Years later Brigadier (Dr) S P Sinha, VSM writing the official history of 8 Mountain Division in the book 'Forever In Operations Volume II' had this to say about the success of this operation:

> "The success of the operation was primarily due to sound planning by the Brigade based on reliable intelligence. The leadership shown by the commanding officer (CO) of 2 JAK RIF was another contributory factor. He moved the troops quickly in response to fleeting situations. The troops displayed a very high standard of fieldcraft and shooting. The performance of young officers was commendable. The approach from different directions took the militants by surprise. The deployment of deep stops was found to be very effective in blocking fleeing militants".

OPERATION HAZRATBAL (15 OCT 1993 - 16 NOV 1993)

Operation Hazratbal was a month long operation conducted by 31 Sub Area with effect from 15 Oct 1993 to 16 Nov 1993. The operation was launched consequent to terrorists taking cover in the Holy shrine that houses the Holy relic of the Prophet. It was well known for some time that terrorists, whenever chased in the area around the Shrine would take cover inside the mosque where they would be safe from the security forces. This was due to self imposed restrictions of security forces of not entering holy places whatever be the provocation.

In the middle of October 1993 the Border Security Force personnel were ordered to lay siege to the Holy shrine when intelligence reports had indicated that the terrorists had planned to take out the Holy relic from the Holy shrine and thus cause embarrassment to the Government as had happened way back in 1964. The BSF immediately laid siege to the shrine. They were soon replaced by troops of 31 Sub Area. The operation started on 15 October and continued for the next one month. The successful conduct of operation resulted in surrender of about 60 terrorists with almost 20 sophisticated weapons. The terrorists were mainly from JKLF and were led by Mohammad Idris, a hardcore leader of the group. The terrorists included a few PAK nationals too.

OP Hazratbal, Oct-Nov 1993

The Operation brought kudos to the Army and to the nation for firm handling of an extremely volatile situation that was capable of exploding and causing embarrassment to the country from international media and particularly from Muslim and western world who were supporting Pakistan on Kashmir.

The Hazratbal is a Muslim shrine in Srinagar located on the southern bank of the Dal Lake. The shrine contains a relic, the Moi-e-Muqqadas believed to be a hair of Prophet Muhammad. The name of the shrine comes from the Urdu word of Hazrat meaning respected and the Kashmiri word BAL meaning place. **Therefore it means a respected place.**

Located on the bank of the great lake, towards the north it has a small stretch of land called Sona Lanka about two hundred meters away which is a narrow piece of land jutting in to the lake. Around the holy shrine are the two Mohallas (locality) called 'Halwai Mohalla' and 'Dhobi Mohalla' which are located towards the East and the West of the Holy Shrine. Two great educational Institutions that is Sher-e-Kashmir University and the Regional Engineering College are located close to the shrine.

According to the legend the relic was first brought to India by Syed Abdullah, a descendent of the Islamic Prophet Muhammad who left Medina and settled in Bijapur in 1685. His son Syed Hamid having been stripped of the family estates by Emperor Aurangzeb sold it to a wealthy Kashmiri businessman Khwaja Nur-ud-Din Eshai. Aurangzeb initially sent the relic to Ajmer to the shrine of Khawaja Moinuddin Chishti, but later sent it to Kashmir. The relic arrived in Srinagar in 1700 along with the body of Khawja Nur-ud-Din Eshai (who had unfortunately died by then). This was received by his daughter Inayat Begum who became the custodian of the relic and she established the shrine. Inayat Begum was married in to the Bandey family of Kashmir whose decedents continue to look after the relic till date. These people are called Nshaandehs.

This relic had gone missing once earlier on 26 December 1963. There were mass protests all over the state forcing the then Prime Minister Pandit Jawaharlal Nehru to make an appeal to the people on 31 December for peace and assured them for early resolution of the issue. The relic was fortunately recovered on 4 January 1964 and the protests subsided thereafter.

On 15 Oct 1993 Lt Gen MA Zaki (Retired), Security Advisor to the State Government, was informed that a large number of terrorists including some top leaders of various tanzims and some mercenaries had taken refuge in the Holy Shrine of Hazratbal. They were believed to have broken the locks of the box containing the Holy relic. A quick decision was taken by the state Government and the Border Security Force (BSF) was ordered to throw a cordon around the shrine to ensure 'Sanctity and Security' of the holy relic. Having deployed the BSF on 15 October 1993, Lt Gen M A Zaki (Retired), next day, decided to requisition services of 31 Sub Area. Accordingly on 16 Oct early in the morning BSF was replaced by 10 GARH RIF, the integral unit of the 31 Sub Area and deployed in Halwai Mohalla which lies to the EAST of the Shrine, where as 6 Maharatha Light Infantry, a Battalion loaned to 31 Sub Area by 56 Mountain Brigade, was deployed in Dhobi Mohalla, this lies to the WEST of the Shrine. 2 JAK RIF which had operated under 31 Sub Area from April 1992 to January 1993 was once again requisitioned and nominated to be reserve and concentrated in Half Chinar, our old location.

On 17 Oct in view of repeated large processions coming to the Holy shrine and firing on our troops from areas surrounding the shrine, 2 JAK RIF was called in and ordered to be deployed around the Holy Shrine to include areas of Naseem Bagh, Habbak and on Sona Lanka in Dal Lake.

We also ensured that all routes to the holy shrine were cut off to the public. Subsequently in view of public reaction to Biz Bihara killings caused by BSF firing on the irate mobs, two more battalions, i.e. 2 SIKH ex 56 Mountain Brigade and 17 SIKH ex 87 Mountain Brigade were also deployed in the city. All residents from 'Halwai Mohalla' locality were evacuated to the hostel of Regional Engineering College and housed there for almost a month. Accompanied by police they were often permitted to visit their houses to collect essential items. In 'Dhobi Mohalla' locality west of the shrine, every morning, people (men only) were collected in a local school and left in the evening. Around the University which housed our unit headquarters, all movement of individuals was kept under control, however complete staff and students who were there in the campus were allowed to move around without any restrictions. The mood of people was quite aggressive in the beginning but it changed over a period of time.

The change of mood was clearly evident one night when, at about 2 AM a couple of professors came and requested us to help one of their colleagues who had suffered a stroke. He needed to be taken to Soura Medical Institute immediately. Despite the fact that there were orders not to move out at night we decided to help them. He was immediately attended to by Captain CM Singh our medical officer, at his residence. The incident had the desired effect on all residents. They all became quite friendly.

We did not look like an occupation force at least in our area thereafter. Meanwhile the entire valley remained shut due to the terrorists call to strike and pull down shutters in support of the those holed up inside the Holy Shrine. The teaching staff and students inside the university campus who continued to stay back, had no problems, their immediate needs were attended to quite regularly. A grocery shop with a rear gate inside a house in Habbak opposite the university campus was permitted to carry on their business with no interference from us.

Our task involved continued vigilance by day and night and to persuade terrorists to give up their struggle without forcing the security forces to undertake the hard option. Various options were considered however, as it turned out the policy to wait and persuade the terrorists to give up proved better. It avoided the bloodshed that was being apprehended all along. Our battalion was tasked to ensure that there was no interference to the Holy Shrine or to the troops guarding it, from outside and secondly to keep the complete area around the Holy shrine out of range of the processionists who almost daily threatened to march on to the shrine and free the terrorists. We formed a ring around the shrine, which helped us to keep every one away. We faced over half a dozen processions. All these processions were handled with absolute restraint but with requisite firmness. No bullets were fired and no injury caused despite grave provocations. Against one such procession the CRPF used about 50 tear gas shells to disperse a mob. They apprehended one of the processionists. On finding them unable to quell the mob we took over the situation and warned the public. They requested that their boy be released. Since there was no serious offence against him we allowed him to go and the situation stabilized.

Though 10 GARHWAL RIFLES and 6 MAHARATHA LIGHT INFANTRY received major portion of the public glare and publicity since they were continuously under the eyes of the press we did convince ourselves and our troops that ours was also an equally important job. We ensured that there was no threat to the shrine what so ever. One of the main reasons the troops of first two units could do their task so well was effective surveillance provided by 2 JAK RIF both by day and night. Everynight all officers including the commanding officer made rounds, of the entire perimeter in turn to ensure that every one was careful in carrying out his duties. We also kept at least three vehicles in front of the Holy Shrine every night which were switched on every half an hour for 15 minutes. With headlights facing the holy shrine they made a lot of noise. While most of us remained awake at night, we also ensured that the terrorists did not rest either.

The continuous vigil of the troops did wear out the terrorists, who finally gave up on 16 November 1993. There was no firing, no injuries and no undue harassment. Public inconvenience was there but it was certainly minimized. Due respect was shown to ladies, old and to the children. It goes to the credit of all troops that not a single complaint was filed against any officer, Junior Commissioned officer or Jawan for any offence, misconduct or misbehavior or even for plucking apples.

The press was there throughout. Mr. Sanyal of Door Darshan did an excellent job, daily covering the happenings of the shrine and ensuring that the same were telecast on the same day. There was a fair amount of interference from civil officials however they were kept at bay successfully by the Sub Area Commander. Some senior Government officials at times tried to give direct orders to Commander however, he stood his ground well and took orders only from his seniors that is the COS/GOC 15 Corps. During the entire episode the Commander stayed in Regional Engineering College and daily visited the troops thereby sharing the difficulties with us. He was readily available and gave immediate decisions when ever approached. It was his perseverance, firm hold of situation, determination and application of humane approach that saw us through.

The Sub Area Commander had tasked us to ensure that by the time we left the area of 'The Holy Shrine' the children of the area must wave at us and wish us good luck. When we came in on 17 October there was clear hostility visible on faces of the complete population including the children. We took up the challenge most earnestly and maintained a very healthy contact with them. On termination of the operation the Commander directed that he should be escorted by CO 2 JAK RIF up to Gupkar road which is close to the Badami Bagh Cantonment, even though we had to go to Manasbal which was in the opposite direction. He could have asked his integral unit to escort him to Badami Bagh cantonment who in any case had to go to the same location. However he chose us for whatever reason he had in his mind. Enroute he saw the children wave their hands with a cheer on their faces, he was visibly very happy and satisfied. He complimented the unit for the excellent performance.

The hardwork of one month by all ranks brought us compliments once again from the Chief of Army Staff as also from the General Officer Commanding in Chief Northern Command and GOC 15 Corps. The Sub Area Commander continued to send us his greetings and good wishes for the next two years from Secundrabad where he went to command the Division. There was a special letter from Lt Gen S Padmanabhan, VSM, then GOC 15 Corps (and later COAS), which amplifies the performance of the unit in this operation very aptly. It is undoubtedly a prized possession that any unit can ask for. This letter and a special message from COAS are attached as appendices.

BLOOD BATH AT PALNO PANDITPURA

"This is the story of a blood bath that took place in the village of Palno Panditpura in South Kashmir on the afternoon of 7 Sep 1994 resulting in elimination of three dreaded militants and recovery of 3 AK rifles. The operation saw martyrdom of four of our brave soldiers in service to the nation. The gun fight left the whole area stunned for days".

The killings in and around village Palno Panditpura in tehsil Kulgam of South Kashmir on 7 Sep 1994 were caused as a result of an afternoon operation launched by us. Our unit had operated in parts of Kulgam tehsil of Anantnag district and Shupian tehsil of Pulwama district for four months in 1993. We were deployed once again in the same area on 1 January 94. Geographically major portion of battalion area of responsibility lay between Rembiara and Vishwa rivers. The entire area was infested with terrorists being a stronghold of Jamaiti activists of Hizbul Muzahideen.

With dawn of 1994 the area had seen terrorism for four years. Large number of Kashmiri youth had been to Pakistan for training. Some of them were trained locally too. By and large all of them fired at us at regular intervals, ambushed us of and on and occasionally fired grenades at our camps too. They saw us carefully, studied our movements and operational patterns and inadvertently were further trained. Our normal pattern of operations was to wake up at 1 AM, leave for operation an hour later, cordon the target village by 5 or 6 AM and return by evening. Terrorists after day break in areas other than our objective for that day, generally relaxed, moved about freely and often laughed at us. It is said that to follow a set pattern of routine in an insurgency infected area is suicidal. So we changed our tactics, started operating by day and night, by foot or transport including requisitioned civil transport and soon thereafter the terrorists were on the run.

Autumn in the valley brings good rainfall, lots of almonds, walnuts and of course apples too. The entire valley is lush green; militarily there is good foliage and cover. During this period we had realised that the terrorists usually left their houses and relaxed in the orchards. They tried taking advantages of the greenery and the foilage. We therefore changed our tactics too. Late in August 1994, taking advantage of same cover we carried out a series of successful operations all in the afternoons on foot, when terrorists probably thought we would be resting. We managed to surprise them, resulting in encounters and their eliminations. In one case a terrorist was caught washing his scooter, and in another, one was returning after meeting his fiancée and in yet another case one was caught after he ran into a school in village Nunmai located south of Yaripura and started teaching the children with a book held upside down. It was in such circumstances that the battalion planned another cordon and sweep operation in gen area Yemrach-Dasyand-Haider Hangir-Palno Panditpura-Manchhu-Hangalbuch and Kathpura on 7 Sep 94. All these villages lie between a square bounded by Yaripura, Chitragam, Imam Sahib and Kadir, about 15 Km west of Biz Bihara.

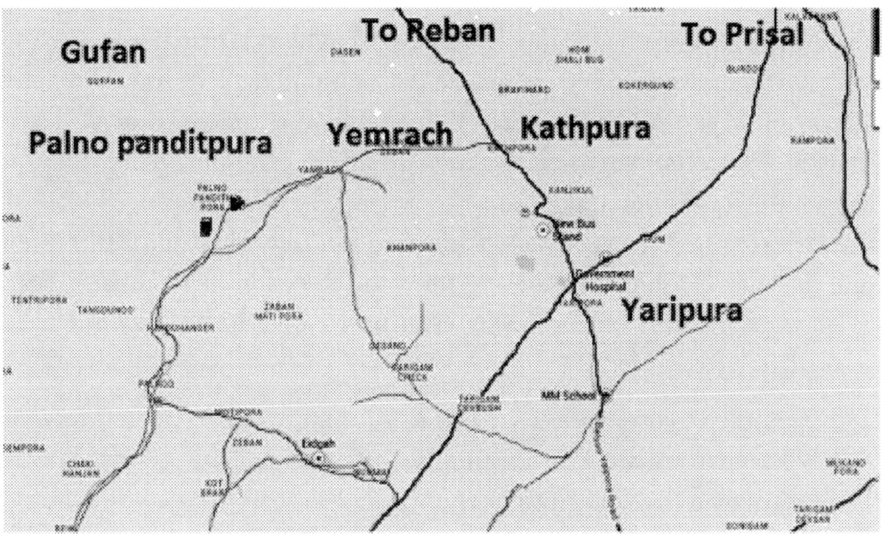

OP Palno Panditpura 7 September 1994

We had reliably learnt that some terrorists had been collecting money from innocent public for the past few days. They were active generally in the day light hours and on that day reported to be in area south west of Yaripura between Yemrach and Palno Panditpura. Commencing at siesta time of 1400 h we planned to sweep the area of apple orchards and concentrate at a village called Yemrach. We had decided to cordon it and carryout a thorough search of the same. The four rifle companies of the battalion were to move from three directions while the commando platoon also called 'Ghatak' platoon, led by 2/Lt RR Tiwari from the fourth. The commanding officer's patrol led by CO and brave 2IC Ghanshyam (also called Ghanu in short) who had just picked up half colonel rank a day earlier and the dauntless Adjutant Lakhi were to dash straight to the village and freeze all movements there. To achieve surprise the commando platoon used a civil hired bus, took off from Prisal in to opposite direction, i.e. towards Arwani lying to north of our base of Prisal. Later they turned towards Babapur on road Arwani-Shupian, came to Chitragam and then to Murad Gufan which was the debussing point for them.

We left our Camps of Prisal, Mammen and Babapur around 1330 h. While the companies commenced their sweep at 1400 h the commanding officer's patrol comprising of two x 1 ton vehicles, two jongas and one ambulance jonga rushed through Yaripura straight to Yemarch. On reaching the objective village, everyone rushed through different streets and ordered all present in the village to freeze. All men folk were ordered out. We learnt that three terrorists at that moment were sitting just outside the village to the south, inside the apple orchards. Seeing the troops inside the village the terrorists tried to get away. While two ran towards Palno Panditpura, one ran into C Company coming from the direction of Nunmai. After a brief firefight the terrorist was eliminated and his AK assault rifle immediately recovered.

The other two terrorists were seen running out of Yemarch towards Palno Panditpura by the commando platoon led by young Tiwari. Incidentally we had two Tiwaris one was Harsh, company commander of a company and the other was Second Lieutenant RR Tiwari leading the commando platoon. We affectionately called him 'Junior (Jr)'. So Jr and his boys chased these terrorists into Palno Panditpura. On arrival Jr divided his patrol in to two sections. Sub Omkar Singh with one section was tasked to enter the village from north while Jr with the other section went around the village and entered the same from south.

Both patrols entered the village stealthily and steadily. Jr and his section as they entered a lane saw two tough looking boys talking to each other. On seeing the troops appear suddenly one of them quickly took out an AK rifle fired at them and tried to run away. Jr fired back immediately dropping him while the other managed to run down the lane. Rifleman

Phula Sherpa a very brave boy with one jawan chased this militant who was seen getting inside a three storied building. Jr tried to speak to the injured militant. Mean while the other militant who had got into a dominating building fired through a window at Jr. The bullets whizzed past him. God was on our side till that moment but he seemed to have changed sides immediately thereafter. A little later the same militant managed to bring down aimed fire at Phula Sherpa who was unfortunately hit. He succumbed to his injuries almost on the spot.

While this fire fight was on, Sub Omkar Singh entered the village from opposite direction with equal care and stealth. They were however not aware about the location of the militant who was hiding in the dominating house. Sub Omkar Singh and his leading scout Rifleman Kharak Bahadur suddenly came under effective fire and both got injured. Rifleman Joginder Kumar of the same section voluntarily stepped forward to evacuate them; unfortunately in the process he got a bullet injury in his neck and succumbed to his injuries too.

Jr meanwhile informed the adjutant at 1640 h about this action and the injuries to his personnel. We ordered him to stay put. Leaving three officers at Yemrach we ran to our vehicles. With Ghanu and the adjutant with one junior commissioned officer and 18 other ranks we immediately rushed to Palno Panditpura in two one ton vehicles. Approach road to this village had earlier been damaged by the terrorists. The last 200 m had to be a dash on foot again. In 35 minutes we were with Jr. Before leaving Yamrach we had instructed Harsh to leave Delta company in that village and rest everyone was to join us at Palno Panditpura. They joined us by 1700 h.

Meanwhile resuscitation of casualties and their evacuation was undertaken. Major M Jogdand was sent off to the hospital with the casualties at 1730 h. We placed Alpha company as inner cordon around the house in which the third militant was hiding and the other two rifle companies on outer cordon around the village to ensure that there was no interference from outside.

At about 1800 h the commanding officer called up Captain Gulshan Chadha to join him alongwith his MMG detachment in a house which was adjoining that occupied by the terrorist. The three storied building in which the terrorist had taken cover had a total of 65 openings (we counted that later), all covered with blue coloured wire mash. These were actually two houses with common first and second floors. The terrorist was constantly changing his windows and therefore it was difficult to pinpoint his location. While we were engaging him with MMG he fired back and hit Havildar Pyar Singh, the detachment commander in the neck. Havildar Pyar Singh was martyred instantaneously. We now moved to yet another room that was even closer. The commanding officer instructed Captain Gulshan Chadha to take out a brick from the wall and make a loophole from where we could try and engage the militant. The militant must have seen the loophole and he fired back at us. Two bullets came through, hit the wall and then ricocheted and hit Captain Gulshan Chadha. Though the bullets had probably lost the momentum but still hit the officer on his right forearm and on the right groin region. At 1830 h, 2/Lt M S Tanwar was detailed to escort Gulshan to the hospital with yet another patrol. We tightened the inner cordon and tried to cover every opening the militant was using, the fire fight continued till about 1930 h. It was beginning to get dark.

At this stage Ghanshyam suggested that we could try and negotiate with the terrorist through the village headmen and advice him to give up or else not only would he be killed, the house would be destroyed too. That would indeed result in unnecessary loss of the life and cause damage to the property. We explained to him that with about 30 or 40 rounds of ammunition left with him he had no chance of survival. He declined the offer. We realized any further delay may give an opportunity to the terrorist to escape. The brave lot comprising Ghanu, Harsh and Lakhi with numerous boys volunteered to dash inside the house to finish the task. Reluctantly the CO permitted four of them to do so. Covering each other they went inside. Charged at the terrorist and fired number of bullets at him. The firefight lasted for about three minutes and it was quiet thereafter.

It was a sad day for all of us. A reprisal from the battalion was definitely expected. Tempers rose high and most of us were fuming. However, better sense prevailed and we controlled ourselves. There was no loss of civil life or damage to any property despite almost four hours of firing. No civilian was hit or injured. This was the first time that though we had killed three dreaded terrorists of Hizbul Mujahideen, there was no jubilation over the incident. Of the three killed terrorists, one was a section commander, second a platoon and the third a company commander. This was the reason for his stubbornness. It was a prestige issue for him. We lost three boys too. Of the remaining, three days later we lost Sub Omkar Singh in the hospital due to excessive bleeding. His loss was a big blow to all of us as was of the other three. They were all selected soldiers who formed part of our Ghatak platoon. They were all brave and extremely dedicated. Sub Omkar Singh was a brave junior commissioned officer and an excellent soldier and a platoon commander. All ranks of the BODYGUARD battalion will always remember the brave JCO and the 'Boys' who sacrificed their lives in selfless devotion and dedication to service and to the country.

'We Salute Them'

A Challenge at Bolus

The challenge at Bolus is a story of an excellent operation conducted by the unit on 31 December 1994 was characteristic of examplary courage, bravery, junior leadership, team spirit and cohesiveness of the unit displayed by all ranks that was duly complimented upon by the Chief of Army Staff. This was an over night operation on the 'New Year Eve' with snow all around resulting in elimination of three dreaded terrorists. We had a major set back in that operation as explained in subsequent paragraphs. Notwithstanding the set back the gallent team of BODYGUARD continued round the clock that night to see that the operation was successfully concluded.

Bolus also called Balsoo is a very interesting place. It lies on the crossroads of road Yaripura-Bugam-Kulgam and Kadir-Buchroo-Khudwani. Wherever we had to go, invariably the route had to pass through this village. And when ever we returned through this village unless the route was secured the terrorists would ambush and fire at us. On one particular day we returned from an operation and halted at the crossroads. There is a general stores shop at this location, the owner probably Nasir Ahmed Wani helped us with chairs and tea which was always paid for. On that day we parked our vehicles facing Yaripura and sent a column of troops on foot to secure the route Bolus-Yaripura and beyond to Prisal.

The moment the route was secured we sat in our vehicles. While the leading column started for Yaripura the CO QRT turned southwards for Kadir and then turned north towards Nunmai. The road then continues to Yaripura. As we entered Nunmai, we saw sudden commotion in the village. People started running in different directions. We saw a man rushing in to a school, one of our Gurkha boys who was chasing that person, saw him enter a class which was full of children. Our Gurkha boy chased the man in to the class room and saw him sitting in the teacher's seat, our boy also noticed that the man was holding a book up side down. That was a clear sign that he was not a teacher. He was wearing a phiren (the loose coat that all men and women wear in the valley). The Gurkha boy immediately put his hand on the phiren and held the AK rifle that was clearly protruding from inside. We quickly brought him out of the class and the school, put him in a vehicle and brought him to our camp. The children in the school made no representation or any noise. So the Balsoo crossroads had become very important for us. This was the second occasion we had succeeded. We were lucky too and the villagers knew that.

In continuation of the saga of bravery the battalion was once again involved in a day night daring operation in village Balsoo (Bolus) on the New Year eve of 1994. Our battalion had continued to be deployed in Prisal, Mamman, Bapur also called Bapapur and in Kaimuh-Khudwani. The battalion had been actively involved in anti militancy operations in this Jamaiti dominated belt since 1992. A large number of terrorists had been neutralized curtsy various infantry and para military units that had been operating in this area from time to time.

By Dec 1994 we had received our move order for move to peace station and had commenced planning to move out of the valley soon. A month earlier the formation headquarters had ordered laying of a Krupmam bridge over the Vishwa river at Kaimuh-Khudwani. Accordingly Bravo company of the battalion under Captain Gulshan Chadha was deployed to protect the bridge and to deny its use by the anti national elements. The battalion was now deployed in four places and therefore its ability to take out troops for anti terrorists operations in area had been considerably reduced.

On 31 Dec, that is the last day of the year 1994 early in the morning, the battalion dispatched a strong administrative convoy for collection of fuel and other stores to depots near Srinagar. A short while later officiating second in command Maj NK Bhatnagar had to leave for the Brigade Headquarters for carrying out a 'Board of Officers' for quarterly check of accounts which had to be done in that year itself. A special patrol of about 20 men all part of CO quick reaction team was sent with him. Therefore after 9 AM only a platoon each was available for operations at Prisal, the Battalion Headquarter location and at Mamman and Bapapur, with no transport except the ambulance vehicle.

Not withstanding the difficulties we decided to strike at the terrorists of Yaripura which lies about 6 Km South of Prisal where we had already had numerous successes. We had learnt that some of the terrorists were visiting a small village called Kanzikul which is about 1 Km away from Yaripura. To the best of our knowledge there was no terrorist left in this particular village of Kanzikul. We also learnt that the terrorists were visiting this small village during the day and sometime had their afternoon meals there. So this was the objective for the Battalion for the last day of the year.

At about 1000 h we commenced our move from Mamman. Lieutenant Maheswar (Manu) commandeered two civil buses, one for himself and second for his commanding officer and came to Prisal at 1030 h. We started from our location in two buses; the first bus besides the commanding officer had Major Harsh Tiwari, SM with Alpha coy less a patrol and our officiating adjutant Captain Vinay Shahi. A patrol from Alpha company was tasked to approach the village from north and with about half an hour gap so as to apprehend any militant who might try and escape. At about the same time Major Thapa with Delta company started from Bapapur in a civil truck and was tasked to approach the village from the west. Short of Yaripura, Manu stopped his bus and sent another patrol through Kokergund to approach Kanzikul from north east. We thereafter rushed in our vehicles through Yaripura almost simultaneously from multiple directions.

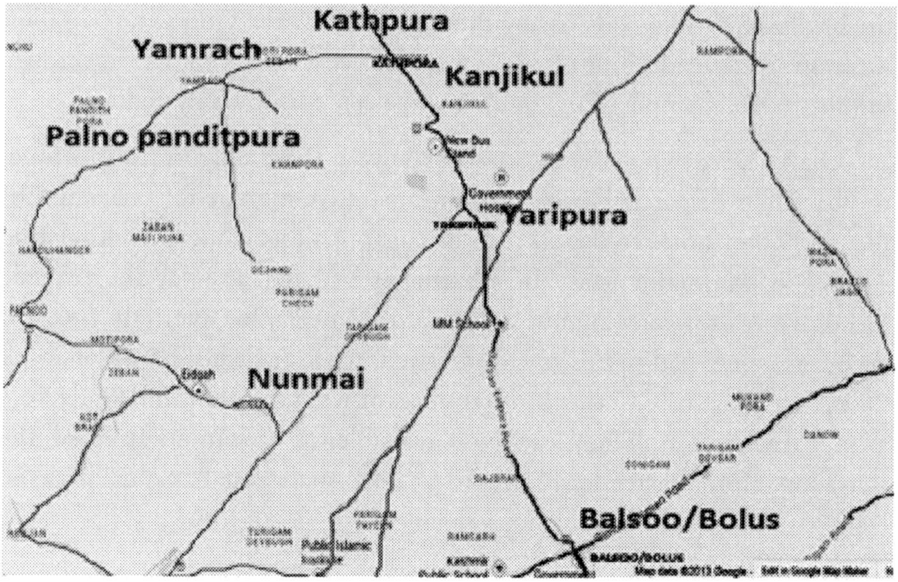

Area of Operations, 31 December 1994
(Village of Bolus is also written as Balsu or Balsoo)

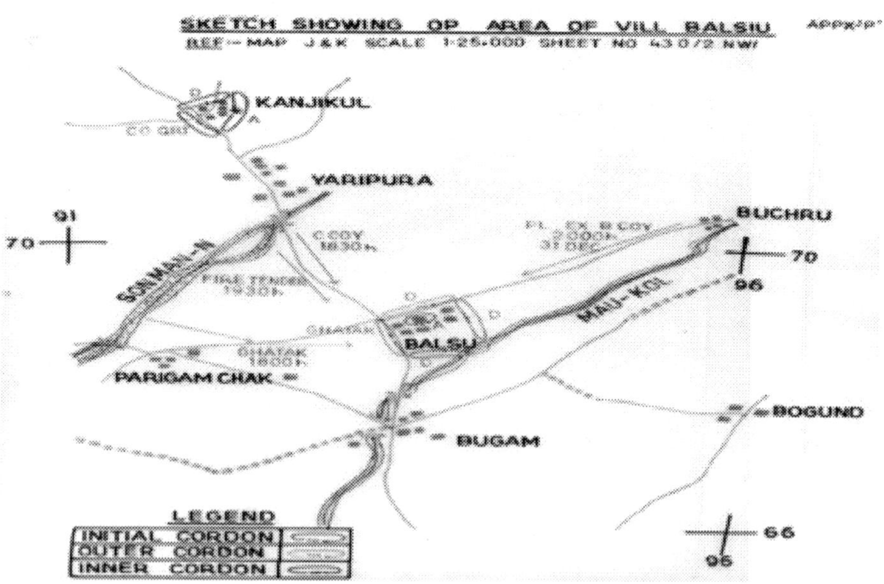

Sketch Showing Operation Area of Village Balsu

Once in Kanzikul we quickly got the men folk together, carried out an identification parade with the help of a guide who took out a terrorist of

Safanagri which lies about a km and half west of Bapapur. During interrogation he revealed information about presence of three terrorists in a particular house belonging to one Gulam Hassan Wani in village Bolus which was 3 km away to the east. Apprehended terrorist revealed that he had met them about an hour earlier. He also informed us that Mr. Gulam Hassan had a hideout inside his house and therefore the terrorists were likely to be present.

Captain Vinay Shahi sought permission of the commanding officer to launch an immediate raid on the suspected hideout. The permission was granted. We sent Manu with 12 other ranks with him. To achieve surprise once again we got hold of a civil bus and the patrol managed to reach their objective without causing too much of suspicion. It was around 1330 h by then. Their movement was so swift that none of the villagers or informers could pass messages about arrival of the troops in the area in time to help the militants or terrorists to get away. Our boys under Vinay Shahi quickly went and surrounded the house.

After ensuring that the house had been properly secured Captain Vinay Shahi entered the house alongwith Manu and one Jawan and of course with the apprehended militant. Without making noise they stepped inside. The first room on the right had some ladies and children sitting and gossiping, the one on the left had three terrorists with two AK rifles resting against the wall. They immediately picked up their weapons and opened fire. There was a total confusion in the house by then. Undeterred, Vinay fired single shots and dropped one terrorist, while the other two managed to enter a room towards the rear of the house. The terrorists continued to fire through the commotion and dust, inside the house. In order to avoid causalities to ladies and children Vinay came out of the house and tried to persuade the terrorists to surrender. Simultaneously he informed the commanding officer on the radio set and apprised him of the situation. Fortunately for us we found a taxi in Kanzikul and with five other jawans the commanding officer rushed to Bolus. By a sheer stroke of luck the commanding officer took one nursing assistant with him. On arrival, the party quickly got off the vehicle, borrowed a fifty rupee note from Nasir Ahmed wani, the shopkeeper, paid to the taxi driver, and quickly ran in to the village and joined Vinay and Manu.

The house had been well covered. The commanding officer was about to tell Manu to climb up on the roof from outside when one of the terrorists threw a grenade from inside the house. Vinay was only five meters from the commanding officer who saw him getting injured. The commanding officer quickly grabbed him and took him to a side. Vinay had been hit by a number of splinters and was bleeding from right side of the forehead near the temple. It did not seem to worry him. He earnestly apologized for having been injured and not completing the assigned task. He however did ask the Commanding Officer to look through his left eye which he said was paining badly. Apparently, everything looked quite all right, the eye was slightly red but nothing else could be made out. It was much later that we learnt of two splinters which had gone right through his eye and had got embedded next to his optic nerve leaving a permanent mark on his handsome face.

Our apprehended militant had also been injured, we caught hold of a bus which had just came from Kaimuh and ordered it to turn around, and evacuated Vinay and the injured militant to Kaimuh. They were escorted by Manu, the CO protection boy and by the nursing assistant. Captain Gulshan who was at Kaimuh was ordered to receive them and to keep a patrol with three vehicles ready to move to the Base Hospital 60 km away at Srinagar. Kaimuh was 6 Km away from Bolus with some of the most notorious villages' enroute. With the limited manpower and no transport at hand some risks had to be taken. Moving them at speed was therefore necessary and probably the only option. Simultaneously orders were issued to Majors Harsh and Thapa to delink from Kanzikul and to join the commanding officer at Bolus. The cordon around the house was tightened. We ordered all menfolk, women and children out of the village so as to avoid casualties to innocent public. In about half an hour both companies arrived in Bolus. We now laid a tight cordon around the house and another one around the village. It was 1600 h by then. We had only about two hours of daylight left. There was a good TV programme of the New Year awaiting in our camps but the operation could not be called off. We tried to negotiate through some civilians and tried convincing the terrorists to see the futility of their fight. We assured them of all help, guaranteed their safety but they decided to fight it out. Of the two terrorists hiding inside one was a company commander of Hizbul Mujahideen and the other a rank and file. They were both from the same village. The one killed was also from the same village. The difference of rank structure ensured that they had to put up a fight and would not surrender. Any way in compliance of their wishes we got them into fire-fight. At about 1900 h the house caught fire which quickly engulfed a triple storied house immediately to its left. All houses in the valley generally store fuel for warming in the top floor which is prone to fire. The terrorists unfortunately for us managed to not only survive but also managed to escape into the neighboring house.

We adjusted the cordon and helped the family members and occupants of the triple storied house to evacuate their belongings. Fortunately for all of us we were able to take out an unfinished silk carpet, a gas cylinder and most of the belongings. Maj Nitin Bhatnagar having finished his job in the brigade headquarters joined us at Bolus around 1830 h. He was quickly sent back to Yaripura to get a fire tender. He was also instructed to walk back from Yaripura so that he would not become a target for the terrorists. He did a magnificent job. Not one but he got two fire tenders. Immediately on arrival, they controlled the fire that had engulfed the next two houses.

Around that time inside Bolus all hell broke lose. There was firing by terrorists from almost every direction, particularly from north and east of the village. Inside the village everyone seemed to be out on the streets, cursing, shouting for withdrawal of Army. A few minutes earlier we had allowed all civilians to return to their houses in view of severe cold and snow. There was over one feet of snow all around. But instead of returning quietly to their homes they decided to create confusion and thereby help the terrorists to escape. Four months earlier in a similar action in Kaimuh a 5000 strong mob had managed to help escape of a dreaded terrorist called 'Man Gublee' from our dragnet. This time we were extra cautious and careful.

Captain Gulshan with two platoons was ordered to rush down from Kaimuh, he had just returned from the Base hospital leaving Captain Vinay Shahi there. Ghatak platoon was requisitioned from our base at Prisal since all administrative convoys had returned to Prisal. On their arrival they were sent to Bugam. Maj Thapa took over the cordon around the village and Maj Harsh Tiwari around the group of houses where the terrorists were hiding. Later this inner cordon was reinforced by Captain Gulshan Chadha. Inside the village we had to fire in the air and scare the men and women to lock themselves inside their respective houses or face dire consequences.

From Prisal the battalion mortar platoon was asked to fire a few illumination bombs at maximum range, this created the requisite scare and interference from inside and outside the village quickly faded away.

In about two hours the situation was brought under control. The firing had died down. The complete neighborhood was quiet and peaceful. The two terrorists hiding inside were safe too and so were their weapons. The CO consulted both company commanders and the junior commissioned officers. A quick evaluation of the situation showed that while we had killed one terrorist his weapon had not been recovered, and while Captain Vinay Shahi was injured, the other two terrorists were still hiding inside with their weapons. It was extremely cold, we had also not catered for dinner, and finally, there was no manpower to spare in the camp that we could call with our dinner without jeopardising the security of the camp. Last but not the least was the New Year programme on the TV to watch. Everyone was of the opinion that we would stay put, food or no food, TV or no TV. So we firmed in wherever we were. It was also decided not to engage the terrorists in further fire fight at night and to wait for the daybreak. It also helped us to avoid creating more confusion and unnecessary casualties at night. We ensured a very tight vigil and gave no chance to the terrorists to escape.

All troops around the target house and on the cordon were allowed to light deliberate fires. This was done so that they could keep themselves warm and create light which increased observation. Since grass was available in plenty we could keep ourselves warm throughout the night. To ensure there was no laxity, all officers carried out patrolling in turn for an hour each. We fortunately had kept a few civilians, both from Balsu and some from other villages who happened to be passing through, for their personal security. They were all accommodated in a house just outside the village, which we requisitioned through the village headman. It was a two bedroom house. All civilians detained for their safety and the owners of the house including ladies were accommodated in one room and we occupied the other, house was well guarded and the owners including the lady members did not object to any inconvenience. They were witness to our movements, which were transparent and quite fair.

Fortunately Nasir the shopkeeper who had given the commanding officer a 50 rupee note earlier in the day was also present in that house. He was asked if he had biscuits in his shop, he said he did, and we bought biscuits worth Rs 1352/-. The entire amount was paid to him the next morning. All ranks were given two packets of biscuits each and were asked to make do with that as dinner that night. All civilians who were forced to spend that night in Bolus with us were also given the same ration at the same scale. Every one including our civil friends were quiet happy and no one raised any objection against the inconvenience or against the emergency ration that we gave them. The year moved on smoothly, we did not or actually could not wish each other 'A Happy New Year', with our Vinay in the hospital and the unfinished task at hand which had taken away all our happiness that night.

Next morning was the first day of the year. We started the day with the public announcement for the menfolk to assemble at 8 AM. They were given adequate time to have their morning bite and it also gave us time to get our breakfast from Prisal and of course the cash too. At about 0900 h our officiating commander HQ 3 Sector Rashtriya Rifles, Col J P S Ahluwalia under whom we had been placed for the past month and a half, arrived at the objective. The commanding officer addressed the public and appealed to them to speak to the terrorists to surrender and not put up any further fight. We on our part assured them their safety. A bit of tough talking and motivation of the public helped us identify their relatives. They were advised to speak to the terrorists and to motivate them to surrender without further fight. First we sent in their relatives but the terrorists did not agree. We then called their respective mothers. The two ladies went inside the house and were with the terrorists for nearly half an hour. They failed to convince them.

When they came out they told us that we could proceed and take necessary action since they had failed to make them see reason and logic. It was extremely sad to see two elderly ladies making such a recommendation. We were confident that the mothers would be able to convince them to avoid the blood shed but that was not to be so, any how we decided to take up the challenge as desired by the terrorists.

The house in which the terrorists had taken cover was now very well guarded. All belongings had been removed with the help of civil population. There were animals inside too; they were also safely brought out. This house belonged to one Mr. Manjoor Ahmed. We did not intend to cause any damage to the house but unfortunately in the ensuing firefight the house caught fire. At about 1445h the terrorists suddenly emerged from the house and tried to escape the cordon. They could only move a few meters. One was a rank and file and could get about 10 meters away while his company commander could move just about 2 meters. Both were neutralized, we recovered two AK rifles with magazines and 65 live rounds.

The damage caused to the house was minimized by quick application of fire tenders. We paid immediate compensation too. The entire village as also people from other villages who spent the night with us were witness to our precautions and self control. Our attempts to obtain surrender of the terrorists had though failed but they were genuine. The public therefore did not raise any hue and cry whatsoever.

Next day we received a message from Chief of Army Staff complimenting the unit for an excellent operation. There were number of messages and greetings from other commanders too. Our Vinay at this time was in the hospital struggling to save his eye. We all prayed for his early recovery. On 2 January we evacuated him in an Indian Airlines flight to Delhi from where he was transferred to the famous eye hospital in Chennai. Vinay still carries the scar with him; his disability not withstanding spirits still remain high as ever, always willing to commit himself for any service to the nation. In 1995 he switched over to Army ordnance corps and decided to start afresh in his service career. His love for the valley continued and like Avtar his senior, followed his footsteps and got married in to a Kashmiri family.

This operation brought us following message from COAS.

Anti militant ops at BOLUS on Dec 31 (.) personal from COAS to all ranks (.) my heartiest congratulations for an excellent ops (.) well done (.) I wish all ranks every success in future

---

CHAPTER 6

Lessons Learnt During OP Rakshak (J&K)

The tenure of our battalion in J&K from April 1992 to April 1995 was truly remarkable and memorable. With numerous successes, honours and awards, compliments and greetings from large number of commanders and senior officers, the unit excelled in every field. While the God Almighty and the DURGE MATA helped us a lot, there were numerous slip ups, narrow misses not only for the terrorists but for our own troops too. Many times we narrowly missed hitting each other. Some boys were careless and accidentally fired on themselves or on to their colleagues. But DURGE MATA indeed saved us from taking fatal casualties. There were occasions when we could locate terrorist hideouts both inside and outside the houses but many a times we failed. Some of our boys were brave and excellent runners. They could easily spot a terrorist from a crowd, chase and nab him but some terrorists did manage to give us a slip. In one case one managed to escape from our custody due to our slackness. There were few more mistakes and therefore there was always a scope to learn and improve.

Leading by Personal Example

Setting personal example by the commanding officer and by the company commanders was definitely the single most important consideration or characteristic seen in performance of the unit. Military history is full of examples of major changes in outcome of battles by commanders setting personal examples of bravery, sacrifice and care that they took in looking after the interests of their troops that they commanded. There has to be visible sincerity of effort on part of commanders at all levels led by the senior most leader or the commanding officer himself. One must not be rigid in life. Orders once issued should be reviewed at regular intervals to ascertain their efficacy and practicability. Anything superfluous needs to be changed immediately. The troops when they see their commanding officer and the company commanders willingly accepting to take risks, their response definitely becomes better. '**Leading by personal example is a match winning factor**' and so is looking after the needs of men which is equally important. The comfort of the men, their rest, food, sanitation, recognition, motivation and awards are all important issues which constantly play on the minds of our men and affect their performance. Therefore each commander needs to personally take interest in doing everything at their disposal to ensure that their troops are adequately trained, motivated, well administered and led by personal example.

Transparency in Functioning

Each Commander has to ensure that he needs to be absolutely fair in his decisions, big or small, approachable and transparent in all actions in his command. He must ensure that he is not only fair but must also appear to be fair. Many a times we hear, people complaining of unfair play and favouritism in many units on issues like posting, promotion, selection of personnel for special duties, assignment of tasks and appointments. There are clear instructions laid down on all such issues and one only needs to follow them. Undue favouritism is the root cause of disharmony, lack of confidence, disrespect and demotivation. Whenever such things take place in a unit their output in almost every field will be low. In a formation some units consistently do well in all competitions securing high positions while there are others who show poor results in practically all activities. If we were to study or critically examine their reasons for their low output, lack of equipment or facilities would rarely be the reason. Invaribly it will be lack of motivation and frustation due to reasons of partiality and favouritism in such units. When a commander is faced with a situation where it is not within his powers to help an individual, then there should be no hesitation in seeking approval from higher authorities. This will help build trust, faith and confidence in command. He must not show that he cares only for few or that he has favourites who alone get looked after, particularly in day to day discharge of duties, and on issues like leave and postings. All these activities must be done in transparent manner. This will help build comradeship in unit.

Professional Competence

This is, of course, one of the most important characteristics that is required for any military outfit. Victory comes only to the brave and a competent set up, which most units of our great army, indeed are. The standard of training in our academies and the regimental centres is generally good. There is no reason to doubt that, how ever it is also true that while most units perform very well, there are a few who do not come up to the expected standards. We feel that the difference lies in professional competence of a commander and his professional integrity or honesty. When it is the job of a CO to train his command and prepare them for war, it is incumbant upon him to do so and ensure that he does it sincerely. Men will generally respect a CO more only if he trains them well and suitably prepares them for the tasks ahead.

Foe example if a unit is moving to a counter insurgency area then he must ensure that all officers, JCO's and NCO's are prepared for the impending task. They must know what is the overall situation like? whom are they going to fight? what are the militant groups? their organisation, equipment in terms of weapons being used, their modus operandi and what measures need to be taken right at the outset to defeat them? All officers and JCO's must also know the existing local restrictions for example, no search of houses at night. They also need to learn the nuances of counter insurgency operations and also the local language or the dialect being used by the insurgents. They also must learn about the legal aspects of counter insurgency operations and various instructions issued by higher headquarters regarding human right violations.

Always Stick to Basics

Counter Insurgency operations are characterized by swift and small scale operations, necessitating strong adherance to basic tactics which we have all learnt during our training. Study of numerous ambushes of security forces reveals that invaribly the cause of loss of equipment and life was due to non adherance of basic tactics which we all know but do not practice. For example, we have all been taught that while on a patrol, no body must either cough, talk or smoke and must remain silent and maintain appropriate distances while marching. There is no reason to be bunching together or talking. **Non adherence of these basic tactics is criminal**. It can result in loss of precious lives. Therefore we need to be both educated in basic tactics as also to ensure their strict implementation. Even if a commanding officer has to function like a sergeant major and ensure their compliance there should be no hesitation in doing that, **it will save lives.**

Counter insurgency operations very rarely demand high level planning and execution, these operations are best done by small teams. They lay greater emphasis on surprise which calls for a very high degree of fieldcraft at all levels. As a rule these small teams must never be sent alone. They must have a support team available with about half an hour gap. Patrols must have different route out and rout in. Where it is not possible to change a route then the route must be secured. One must never try and get back from an operation in a hurry, if we do that we are asking for trouble. Routes of return journey must be invaribly secured. Finally we must be alert and never follow a set routine. Routes, timings (in terms of day or night operations), mode of transport etc, must all be changed regularly. Working on a set pattern is again asking for trouble. We must constantly review our conduct of operations and when ever required changes must be made so as to improve our performance. It would not be incorrect to say that we could also learn from the militants which will helps us take suitable corrective measures.

Courage of Conviction

Forcing change is generally known to be difficult; there is usually resistance to change. This is equally applicable in operational matters as also in our day to day life. We normally do not wish to disturb the existing system for the fear of failure and our unsubstantiated concerns. However when we find that the change is inevitable and is necessary, then the commander has to take a stand to order the change and ensure its implementation. On assumption of command, the commanding officer was advised to control consumption of alcohol. We found that on sundays there was Tambola in the unit, which was quite fine but alongwith that, was uncontrolled sale of rum, which had to be stopped. Some senior officers even cautioned us that there could be a revolt in case if we did that. Troops were explained that we were in thick of anti militancy operations where they were expected to remain alert and avoid consumption of alcohol altogether. In any case there were orders that only one peg would be permitted on sundays in the afternoon only. We decided to enforce that despite resistance from some quarters. This was a small issue but an important one that affected our performance in operations. The results followed soon thereafter and the troops accepted the change willingly. Another change that we ordered was carrying of packed food instead of cook houses for operations. We had seen that when we carried the cook houses for preparing hot lunch, there was at times undue diversion of focus from operations. We therefore ordered that henceforth every one would carry packed lunch and the cook houses would not be carried any more. This order was also contested by officers. We explained to every one in detail and thereafter forced its implementation with astounding successes.

Operationally we had the freedom to choose our objectives which was based on our ground intelligence, interaction with the apprehended terrorists and the civil population. Sometimes objectives were decided on mere appreciation of the movements of terrorists. These objectives were coordinated and approved by the Brigade Headquarters. At times there was a tendency to choose easy targets rather than difficult ones, particularly where climbing of hills was involved. When ever we did that we realized that the areas that were not addressed the militants tended to shift into that area. This was probably the reason why militants concentrated in Sopur and later in Hill Kaka in Poonch district. We had therefore taken the decision that we will address the complete area and would not let the militants concentrate anywhere, no matter how difficult the area or the terrain was.

Conduct of Ground Training and Firing

"More you sweat in peace less you bleed in war", is an old saying known to all soldiers, but not always seriously practiced. This is what we need to do. No matter how busy one is, time has to be taken out for training of troops in minor tactics, firing of personal weapons, training with new equipment, and learning local language/dialects. We need to train on ground rather than spending too much time in class rooms. While it would be correct to give preliminary talk or introduction in class rooms but emphasis must always be on practical training on ground.

Time needs to be allocated for discussing each operation, good or bad and learning from mistakes made there in. It will help in understanding reasons for the failure and enable remedial actions. Officers and JCO's could also suggest change in tactics or in conduct of these operations. In a counter insurgency operational area, training of troops assumes greater importance. It not helps improve our military skills it also shows to the public that the body of troops conducting training are serious soldiers, who are constantly trying to improve. These activities are seen by the public and conveyed to the anti national elements. They will think twice before engaging such troops. Conduct of firing practices also helps in improving a soldier's ability to shoot accurately with speed and builds his confidence in his weapon systems. It also helps him in testing his weapon before going in to operations.

Collation of Intelligence

This is an essential pre-requisite for launching of any operation. For success in war it is necessary to know one's opponent, his capability and characteristics, his training, his sustainability and his strength and weaknesses, all these need to be correctly analyzed. Information about the terrorists and anti national elements in counter insurgency operations can best be obtained from the public itself. In other words we need to cultivate the civil population. And the best way is to treat them genuinely well, we need to look after their needs and avoid being a bully. They will certainly respond. Interaction by the doctors and medical staff can yield good results. Taxi drivers by virtue of their frequent travel and meeting large section of society can be a good source of information and intelligence. Developing friendship and offering them help once in a while, proved extremely beneficial. On many occasions while travelling in a taxi the driver would certainly stop in front of a group. That used to be an indication that the group contained some friends that we were looking for. That was enough and we would finish the job. In some cases we found that the drivers would very smartly warn the terrorists by blowing horn in specific manner like blowing twice or three times. They were thus able to unsuspectingly caution their friends. Such people had to be suitably warned.

We need to develop an intelligence grid at company and battalion level. Details of militants of each village with complete details must be recorded and collated at battalion level. It will help in maintaining a record and enable tracking of their movements, through their parents, friends and relatives. Obtaining intelligence through military means that is through electronic surveillance and radio interception, information from higher headquarter, study of pattern of operations and movements of terrorists also provides actionable intelligence. All these activities need to be taken seriously. Actionable Intelligence needs to be acted upon immediately and without loss of time, otherwise the entire effort is wasted. We saw that in many operations particularly in Waltuyiang on 5 May 1993 and two months later in Turkpura as also in Operation Alpine Noose. In all these cases we reacted in minutes and were able to successfully eliminate large number of terrorists.

Our sources need to be protected. Their safety and security is extremely important. Should their identity be compromised, not only would we lose the sources others would also not come up to help the security forces. The contact men or man in the unit must be limited to one or two individuals only. Though the contact man could best be the commanding officer or his second in command or the adjutant, however it would not be incorrect to detail a suitable NCO like we did nominate late Havildar Nek Singh to interact with the sources since he was conversant with the local language and knew the people and terrain very well. The aim of this exercise is that such interactions must be limited to as few people as possible. This would increase the survivability of the sources.

Involvement of All Stake holders in Planning of Operations

In counter insurgency operations young officers and junior leaders must be consulted in selecting and planning of operations. With their ground knowledge and experience they would be in a good frame of mind to plan and conduct such operations. This will also encourage all officers to participate wholeheartedly in conduct of each of these operation. We allowed our adjutants invariably to plan such operations. They would plan, get them approved from the commanding officer and then issue the necessary orders. We found that the system worked extremely well. Each and every officer worked with enthusiasm, led their troops with personal example in a bold and a courageous manner. On one occasion we had the privilege of two reporters from France who accompanied us for an operation along the Wular lake in September 1993. They were involved in the planning and the actual conduct of the operation. In their brief published in the media abroad, they wrote a magnificent review of what they saw. They were visibly impressed with the performance of Indian troops.

Dynamism in Conduct of Operations

Our training manuals on counter insurgency operations lay elaborate guidelines for conduct of operations against the terrorists or the anti national elements. These guidelines are generic in nature and need to be modified depending upon the terrain, area, type of terrorists and weapons being used by them. During our operations in the valley we realized that the terrorists, who were either trained by Pakistani handlers or trained by local cadres, were inadvertently trained by the security forces as well. The terrorists regularly saw our activities, our movements and conduct of operations. We also realized that the youth in the valley were generally very intelligent and observant and learnt a fair degree of tactics from us. We therefore had to regularly change our tactics, routine, timings, mode of transport and even our attire when required. We tried to learn from their tactics too. In 1993 we realized that whenever we approached a village some one would fire a round in the air and warn every one of our presence. In our first operation after shifting to Prisal in March 1993 we did the same. Harbans the second in command was asked to enter the village and fire a single round from his AK rifle. The moment he did that we caught a tough looking bearded guy at half past four, that morning wearing a black track suit and good quality sports shoes . His attire revealed his identity. He promptly gave us two AK rifles and six magazines with 180 rounds of AK ammunition.

Initially when ever we went out for an operation, most of us would sit around and light fires to keep ourselves warm. Every one including the civil population saw where we were standing or sitting, the terrorists would comfortably get adequate time to prepare and hide and we would invariably go back in the evening empty handed. We changed this routine. Every one was clearly told that there would be no fires lit till one hour after the first light. The order was strictly followed and soon we started getting good results. We had overall 25 percent success rate in our operations. Nearly 190 out of 581 operations that we carried out in our complete tenure were successful in either a recovery of weapon or a killing or capture of a terrorist.

We got four burqas (worn by muslim ladies) stitched, but did not use them. Though we asked the tailors in Prisal to make them post haste, but did not collect them for many days. The word very soon spread around that we were planning to use them. Major General R S Mavi, AVSM, SC our General Officer Commanding 8 Mountain Division, during one of his visits later told us that the terrorists had asked the locals in our area to not to wear burqas for three months. It was after his visit to the unit that he understood the reason for such an order by the militants. These activities did put in a fair degree of pressure on to the terrorists.

Our use of hired transport also created a scare in the area. There were numerous successes that we achieved by use of taxies, buses, trucks and matadors. Every single driver was paid and a clearance taken from them. We constantly changed our conduct of operations. When night operations became routine we switched over to afternoon operations and again achieved good results. Many terrorists were caught either resting, bathing and some washing their scooters and motorcycles. Our experience clearly taught us that the conduct of operations must be constantly reviewed and necessary changes brought about.

Small Team Operations

Anti militant and anti terrorists operations are characterized by small scale operations. While small scale operations are easy to plan, quick to launch and can surprise the terrorists, on the contrary large scale operations are time consuming in their planning, preparation and execution. Large movements are difficult to hide, and this is compounded by limited roads and tracks and improved radio and mobile connectivity. Terrorists get adequate warning and are generally able to take defensive measures. Large scale operations generally end up as wasteful exercises, their failure often demotivates the troops and on the contrary emboldens the terrorists. During our tenure most large scale operations failed however some succeeded too. Our operation in Tral in February 1993 failed but the one in Kaitson on 15 July 1993 was a big success, we were able to eliminate the Deputy commander in chief of the dreaded Hizbul Mujahideen along with over half a dozen terrorists. Our Brigade level operation in Erin bowl of Bandipura tehsil in August 1993 again failed but a few days later in Malangam bowl on 6 October 1994 was a big success again. In a four battalion operation we were able to eliminate 24 terrorists. Later in the next two months large scale operations were conducted successfully in eliminating terrorists from Hazratbal and later in Sopur on 27 November 1993. We realized that large scale operations needed deliberate planning and preparation otherwise they would generally fail.

Our small team operations on the contrary gave us numerous successes. When ever our battalion operations failed we immediately launched a small team operation and it, invariably succeeded. We had also experienced that when ever we went away from our base every one in about two to three hours would come to know of our location. Thereafter the terrorists were free to roam about wherever they wanted. For the Erin bowl operation in August 1993 we left a small team behind consisting of our adjutant and Ashish Maini. They launched a quick operation late in the evening towards the banks of the Wular lake where in a brief encounter they neutralized a Pakistan trained terrorist. In many operations our teams succeeded in surprising the terrorists and over powering them. There how ever was one important point that one had to keep in mind. These teams were themselves vulnerable because of their small numbers. We therefore ensured that they carried adequate ammunition and more importantly a support team always followed them with an half an hour gap. This ensured that the main team was never out of fire power and support. We would invariably also a keep a rifle company ready to be launched at short notice.

Motivation

During the period of operations in 1992-1995, we were all expected to operate every day, targets were in plenty. Every single village in the valley had 5 to 20 youth who had taken up arms. Over 30000 were believed to have gone across the Line of Control to get trained and armed. Most of them came back successfully fully equipped to fight the government machinery. How had such a large group gone across is a different story and not being discussed. Daily operations meant no rest, no time to maintain our equipment and of course little or no time to wash clothes by the troops. Line communications, long distance trunk dialing as also the mobile phone connectivity of today were not available. The troops had little time to write letters back home. Under these circumstances the morale was not expected to remain high during the complete tenure of the unit. This effected the performance of the individuals and therefore of the complete unit. This menace had to be checked, and checked urgently. We therefore had to ensure, not withstanding the difficulties, the "out put" had to be high as expected from a good unit. A number of small issues that effect the morale were taken up. While we passed strict orders not to light fires early in the morning both for warming themselves as also for preparing tea, we went ahead and bought big steel flasks and gave it to each platoon so that they could carry hot tea in it.

The Commanding officer encouraged each officer to set example of professional honesty, fairness and a high degree of integrity. If every one was ordered to carry packed lunch every day we ensured all officers did the same. It was decided to award cash incentive to troops for excellence in operations and in courses of instructions. The amount earlier earmarked for excellence in Army courses of instructions was doubled. The award for excellence in operations in every Sainik Sammelan became an important event where the hardwork of the men was duly recognized. We also decided to promptly initiate citations for all individuals who displayed gallantry and distinguished service in operations. A total of 127 citations were initiated in response to various acts of gallantry in a period of three years. There were over 190 operations which resulted in apprehension/elimination and recovery of arms and ammunition. It was a great honour to receive 86 gallantry awards besides a citation from Chief of Army Staff and an 'Appreciation' from General officer commanding in Chief Northern Command. In many cases there were instances where more than one citation was sent for one individual. All honours and awards were a big incentive for raising the morale of the unit and thereby its overall performance.

Honouring Unit Traditions

This was another aspect that affected the morale and motivation of the unit. It was felt that every commander must honour the heroes and martyrs of the unit or an organization that he commands. He must also honour his predecessors. One may not agree with everything that his predecessor did and therefore may bring about changes, however these must be done without any criticism. We need to keep in mind that the working conditions vary for everyone and these must be appreciated. It has been seen that criticizing the predecessor, demotivates the other members of the unit and also adversely affects the morale. This is more so if the incumbent is not originally from the same unit or the organization. We always paid homage to our heroes and martyrs and felt that paying homage to them made a substantial difference. It also helped us to learn from the experience of elders and veterans in the unit. In numerous pure caste units of our Army officers are known to be fully participating in their religious activities even though it is not followed in their own religion. By well laid down norms the religion of men is the religion of officers. Wherever these things are followed the bonhomie between officers and the men is generally greater which assists in building comradeship and trust.

Discipline

Discipline has an important bearing on the level of motivation of any outfit. While on the face of it, one may say that discipline has no bearing on the morale and motivation, but that is not correct. In case of indiscipline in any unit morale of that unit is definitely affected. The output of such a unit with indiscipline and low morale is bound to be low. Conversely a unit with good standard of discipline is bound to do very well in both war and peace. As commanding officer one had to be strict in ensuring adherence to orders and instructions. Though most troops realized the importance and implications of operations being conducted, there were some who refused to listen and had to be strictly dealt with. In a few cases people did not understand that they were in a serious business, and had to be punished. The message did go around the civil population too. People realized that we were equally strict and fair with our own troops as much as with the anti national elements. Most troops were very positive in their outlook which helped us maintain high morale and motivation in the unit.

Team Work

Wars are always won by combined efforts of all components of the war machinery of a nation. They are not won by individuals. Except for games and sports where individual effort is involved, in every activity that we do, it is the team effort which gets us to the top. Whether it is a soccer match, or a game of hockey or a cricket match, it is the team effort that wins or loses the day. Similarly in every operational task it is the effort of the complete team that ensures success. How do we create the team effort or the team spirit? we felt it wasn't difficult at all, the commander or the commanding officer has to lead personally, ensure genuine concern for training, man management, administration and welfare of troops. Operationally at the level of a unit and below the commanding officer must command his troops by personal example. He must not command sitting inside his operations room. He has to show that he takes part in each and every activity without over worrying for his personal safety. Lets all remember that we die only once, lets do that for the glory of our nation. We must also remember that death can take place anywhere, even in the safety of one's bedroom therefore one must not over worry on this account.

In one of the first 'Sainik Sammelan' (a formal address of troops) taken by the commanding officer after taking over, it was announced that whenever we were fired upon, the company commander was expected to move out immediately and without waiting for clearance or orders, and take offensive action against the terrorists. Troops were told that should any individual of the unit be fired upon, every available officer, JCO and jawan was to immediately pick up his weapon and take offensive action against the attackers, with or without clothes or shoes. On one such occasion the commanding officer came out of the camp in sleeping suit with an AK rifle in his hands. There were two outcomes to this order, firstly, the message went through to the civil population and through them to the terrorists that this unit would react very fast should they be fired upon. Though initially the militant did fire on our camps but it stopped very soon. We repeatedly experienced this wherever we moved to for example in Prisal, Safapura (Manasbal) and once again in Tral the militants stopped firing on our camps within a week or two. Secondly the troops realized that all officers, JCO's and the men were fighting together for one cause and that they were prepared to risk their lives in protection of their colleagues.

Our attempt at sharing hardships with the men including, staying in tents even in winters with snow all around, carrying packed food and not lighting fires despite extreme cold brought all of us closer. Many a times the CO or the adjutant was right ahead while chasing the militants. Troops never objected to numerous hardships that we faced in the complete tenure. On many occasions when our meals could not reach us in time, they did not mind eating biscuits that we all shared. Thus sharing of hardships indeed brought the unit closer. The Brigade staff would often say that 2 JAK was truly a close knit unit.

Trust Members of the Team

One good thing that has come down in the Indian Army from our forefathers is the **trust** we have been trained to develop both for our seniors as well as for the juniors. No matter how difficult a task is assigned, to any officer junior commissioned officer or a jawan, we rightfully expect him to carry it out to the best of his ability and without undue consideration of his personal safety. The Chetwood quotation of "Our Personal safety comes last always and everytime", is always kept uppermost in mind. We must always remember that it is "The Nation", "Soldier" and then self, in that order, always and every time. A soldier looks up to his commander for directions and orders, he is taught to believe that everyone in the unit and upwards will also carry them out with similar zeal. It is only with that conviction and trust a soldier or a young officer will move forward in to the line of fire. The success in Kargil operations in 1999 clearly showed that our young officers and JCO's sacrificed their lives with this conviction. Their bravery and sacrifice brought about glory to their families, their unit and to the Nation.

Some of the important measures that need to be taken by all commanders in order to develop trust are, firstly training of all ranks, developing confidence in their command, their tactics and their weapon systems. This is the most important issue. Second point for developing trust is the fairness in functioning of command, assigning them their duties with out any kind of prejudice. Though this comes in the realm of 'Administration' and 'Man management' however it is equally important, as important as the issue of training. Apart from promising them the moon a commander must take it upon himself to ensure that every thing that is possible and available under the roof must be provided. Each officer, junior commissioned officer and soldier must be fully convinced that his commanders are with him. Each man must be given an opportunity to accept responsibility to train and administer. Junior leaders must be encouraged to make purchases when ever required. Many of us sometimes feel that our juniors can not be trusted with money. In fact money is one issue that generally creates mistrust. Many senior officers do not trust their young officers or junior commissioned officers with financial transactions. We experienced that this was not a correct approach. Let us work with the assumption that most people are honest, god fearing and truthful and given a chance and guidance every one can rise up to the expectations of our great organization.

One of our colleagues once told us that he could not trust his company commanders and therefore did not give them any money for any operational task or for the administration of his troops. We advised him that he had to trust his company commanders. The best thing to do was to give them money in front of his junior commissioned officers, and tell them for what purpose that was being given. In case he found that the particular individual did not adhere to his instructions then he as commanding officer should take suitable action against him. It is strongly felt that development of trust is an essential prerequisite for building up team spirit and comradeship.

Volunteering For Operations

Against the common perception that 'never volunteer for anything in the army', which is done to avoid extra work or fatigue, sometimes the proposal looked good but we soon realized that in life unless you volunteer you get no opportunity. And without an opportunity there is no success in life. We joined the Army to serve the motherland and you cannot serve the motherland by just sitting on the ground. Within the limits of sanity a commander must volunteer to carry out difficult tasks. Casualties will of course be there but if we follow our teachings properly they can be minimized. In the valley we volunteered for many such operations and one such was the Sopur operation of 27 November 1993. We overcame three delay lines set up by the militants, neutralized seven and recovered five AK rifles in the bargain. There were two minor casualties, with the blessings of the God Almighty both rejoined the unit in a few days, fully fit to continue with the operations. To add to our achievements was a remarkable message from the Army Commander. Though he had complimented the entire Division that participated but singled out our unit for the outstanding performance that was displayed. This was the price we paid to receive the historic complimentary message from the Army Commander. It is therefore our strong conviction that all of us should be ready to take up any assignment no matter how difficult it is. Every opportunity must be taken up boldly. We may not always succeed but attempt must be made. Let us remember that success will come only to those who at least make an attempt to achieve something in life.

Relations with Civil Population

This was an important aspect that effected our conduct of operations. By and large we saw that no one would help us with any useful piece of information. In a few occasions our individual contacts would pass on some inputs that would help us. Normally it was the conduct of our troops that effected the response from the public. Sometimes inter personal rivalries did help us in gaining inputs about the hostile elements. There were times when we saw no movements in the field, and lack of movement indicated trouble. This was in the form of Improvised explosive devices or an ambush particularly when we were returning from operations. As long as the ladies and the children were out working in the fields there was no danger. Our instructions to troops were to provide immediate help to anyone requesting for assistance, without waiting for clearance. They were advised not to show such assistance as a favour but to do that with genuine concern for elders. We would often remind every one to treat all elders with due care and respect, particularly when they were assembled during operations. Troops were also told to visualise their own kith and kin sitting in the congregation and how exactly would we treat them then? Assistance in removing broken down vehicles and provision of medical aid was highly appreciated. Both Captain Amit Chatterjee and Captain C M Singh our medical officers did a commendable job in providing first aid to civil population particularly in extreme winters when roads were closed due to rain and snow.

Assistance to public helped us gain support from them as also from the administration. In one such case when the road Yaripura-Kulgam was damaged at Bugam by the terrorists we got it repaired with help of young boys from the same village. The terrorists damaged that twice again but each time it was repaired by the villagers voluntarily, of course under our supervision. We also told the villagers that we would not allow the road to remain cut off for more than 24 hours and that it would be repaired by the villagers only. The terrorists stopped interfering with that thereafter. Operation Sadbhavna projects had just been launched. We provided sports equipment and toilet facilities for boys and girls to two schools even though one of them was known to be fermenting anti national feelings among the children. As outcome of our relations with the public there were no complaints against our troops even when we were at fault. We therefore realized that it was extremely important to have good relations. Undue harassment of the old, women and children must be avoided, otherwise it would unnecessarily create more enemies and would be detrimental to the overall interest of the operations.

CHAPTER 7

My Team

The results that the BODYGUARD Battalion achieved in its three years tenure in the peak period of insurgency in J&K between 1992-1995 was undoubtedly a joint effort of all its brave officers, Junior Commissioned Officers and the magnificent men that formed the great unit. The huge successes achieved by the unit were due to the team effort of all ranks who selflessly devoted their energies in carrying out the tasks assigned to them. There were a total of thirty officers who contributed to the Battalion's success and achievements in this tenure. The efforts of both, the senior officers as well as young officers from services who joined us for short periods were commendable. There was intense harmony between officers and the men. Every one willing to live and fight for each other. There used to be a rush for volunteers who opted to lead through the operations. Some would even advise and direct the commanding officer at times not to move ahead of the men. On numerous occasions all of us ran chasing terrorists without over bothering for the chain of command or the dangers involved. It was for this reason that the team clicked and clicked very well.

Col J S Chandel, VSM was the commanding officer when the unit was inducted in to the valley. He had taken over the command of the unit in April 1989 in Sri Lanka during 'Operation Pawan'. He successfully led the battalion through its balance tenure there as also in Lucknow and in 'Operation RAKSHAK' in Punjab during 1991-92. In the valley he was instrumental in training and preparing the unit, launching in to operations and achieving the initial successes. He was affectionately called 'Doctor' due to his expertise in homeopathy. During his tenure as commanding officer of the unit in the valley, over two dozen weapons were recovered and a similar number of terrorists apprehended. He handed over the command of the unit on 15 January 1993 to Lt Col A C Soneja in Half Chinar. He was posted to 87 infantry Brigade as 'Deputy Brigade Commander'. He superannuated on 31 May 1997 after a glorious innings of 28 years of distinguished service. Two of his children are back in Army life, while Ranjit, his son joined as commissioned officer in BODYGUARD in September 2001, younger daughter Sanju married Colonel Neeraj Rana who retired as Principal Himalayan Mountaineering Institute Darjeeling recently. Colonel J S Chandel, VSM has settled down in Bilaspur.

Major Harbans Singh Gill served the unit as 'Second in Command' for nearly two years. A very bold, brave and a committed officer, Harbans was instrumental in numerous successes achieved by the unit. In April 1993 he, as officiating commanding officer, led an operation in Damal Hanzipura, wading through the icy cold waters of Vishwa River and surprised the terrorists. Five of them were neutralized and five weapons recovered. His contribution in Operation "Waltyingu" and "Alpine Noose" was commendable. Despite having been injured in Yaripura on 4 July 1993, he rejoined the unit as soon as he was discharged. He was tough with the terrorists as also sometimes with the public. In the middle of 1994 he was posted to Rajasthan. He like Colonel J S Chandel, the first CO motivated his son Ajit to join the BODYGUARD as a commissioned officer. Harbans has settled down in Chandigarh.

Major (now Lieutenant General) Ghanshyam Singh Katoch joined the unit in 1992 and served for complete three years in the valley. An illustrious officer, very brave, bold and dynamic company commander from an illustrious family. Contribution of Major Ghanshyam Katoch in successful conduct of numerous operations was commendable. He commanded Alpha Company which was responsible for the first neutralization of a terrorist by the unit in June 1992. That was the beginning and thereafter there were many more. He successfully led operations in Lariyar and Dadsura in February-March 1994, and another one in Srinagar in July 1994 that resulted in recovery of 17 weapons. He was awarded a commendation card by COAS for this operation. He contributed immensely in elimination of terrorists in Operation Alpine Noose on 6 October 1993 and in Palno Panditpura on 7 September 1994. He has excelled in service, commanded 9 JAK RIF, a Brigade and a Division all in counter insurgency areas. He is today commanding a Corps in the western sector. Married to Geeta the couple have one son Giri Raj who is a software engineer.

Major (now Colonel) N K Bhatnagar rejoined the unit in Manasbal in September 1993 after finishing his tenure as Brigade Major in an infantry brigade which was colocated with the unit in the same area of south Kashmir. An extremely competent and a mature officer he briefly commanded the Delta Company and on posting out of Major Rajesh Sood he took over Charlie company. Starting with Operation Alpine Noose he participated in number of successful operations including the famous month long Hazrat Bal operation. He continued to excel in service, commanded the same unit in Arunchal Pradesh. He has settled down in Indore where he worked in real estate sector for about six years. Married to Renu, the couple have two daughters who are happily married.

Major (now Colonel) Rajesh Sood commanded Charlie company which earned good results in operations in all areas that the company was deployed. In operation ALPINE NOOSE on 6 October 1993 it was his troops who picked up the terrorists movements at first light and engaged them by fire, neutralizing the first two and recovering two AK-47 rifles. In south Kashmir the company was deployed overlooking the village of Mammen which was enroute to unit headquarters at Prisal, Dominating the plains of Arwani, Charlie company did a commendable job in providing security to our vehicular columns. Rajesh superannuated in January 2012 and has settled down in beautiful environments of Shimla. Married to Doctor Sanju, the couple have two children. The elder Aishani is undergoing a course in hospital management in Tata Institute of Social Sciences in Bombay and the younger Anish is doing his Engineering in Vellore.

Major (now Colonel) MNH Hussain (also called MNH) joined us in the valley in second half of 1994. A very mature, competent and an intelligent officer, MNH had also operated in Sri Lanka. He guided all of us in smooth conduct of operations in the valley. He was a local officer, therefore knew the people and their problems very well. Conscious of his personal security and that of his family members, we rarely involved him in operations but took active help from him in all aspects of our interaction with the public. He was also tasked to lead our 'Advance party' to our next peace station where once again he credited himself very well. He is married to Rohilla. They have two children, while the elder, Munir is in the Hotel industry; daughter is persuing dental studies and will be a surgeon very soon.

Major (now Brigadier) Harsh Tiwari, Sena Medal rejoined the unit in 1992 after a stint in the NSG. A commando trained officer Harsh was awarded Sena Medal for bravery and distinguished service in Punjab. Therefore by the time he joined the unit in the valley he was already well trained and fully geared up to undertake anti terrorists operations. During the tenure he attended the prestigious Technical Staff Course in Pune which is equated to 'Staff Course' in Wellington. On completion, he volunteered to return to the unit. His contribution has been highlighted in the text of this book. He was instrumental in getting numerous successes including the one in Batmaloo on 29 November 1992 and at Bolus on 31 December 1994. After this tenure he was posted as DQ in a formation Headquarters in Lucknow. He later switched over to Defense Research and Development Organization (DRDO) where in he has continued to rise up. He is already a Brigadier and sitting approved for the next rank and therefore well placed for higher appointments within the DRDO.

Major (now Col) Mahesh Thapa affectionately called 'Kancha' joined us in October 1994 while the unit was in Prisal. He spent about three months in Prisal and another four in Tral. A very brave officer who participated in numerous operations during his short tenure with the unit in the valley. In our Operation Balsu on 31 December 1994 he volunteered to spend the night on snow when two terrorists were holed up inside a house. It was due to the perseverance of the unit personnel in which he formed part that enabled the neutralization of these two terrorists after nearly 24 hours of operation. On 10 March 1995 he was once again accompanying the CO when we confronted a dreaded terrorist in village Turk Tashlu along the Vishwa river. The Hizbul Mujahedin militant was neutralized in a neat operation without suffering any casualty. Mahesh superannuated from the service two years ago and is presently posted in NDA Khadakvasla as a re-employed officer. Married to Deepa the couple have two daughters.

Major (now Colonel) Sandeep Datta joined us in Prisal in September 1994 from High Altitude Warfare School, Gulmarg. A very competent and a brave officer, he opted to join the unit from a difficult area very well knowing that he could well have gone to a peace station after having done a three year tenure in Gulmarg. He joined the unit and served for about eight months in the valley. He participated and led numerous successful operations against the terrorists both in the Prisal area as well as in Tral where we shifted in January 1995. In one of the last operations in Tral he led his company alongwith the CO QRT deep in to the Tral valley resulting in apprehension of two terrorists and recovery of two weapons. It was a complete night operation involving a walk of over twenty km. The success in the operation and compliments from the GOC next day more than made up for the rigours of the night before. Sandeep went on to perform very well in the unit, attended the prestigious Staff Course at Wellington and commanded the BODYGUARD once again in operational areas of Poonch and Rajouri districts of J&K in 2003-06. He took premature retirement from service in 2008 and has settled down in Gurgaon looking after one of the biggest malls in the country. Married to Reena they have one daughter who is persuing her post graduate studies from Noida.

Major (now Colonel) RSK Nair was posted as Delta company commander when we joined the unit in November 1992. A tall slim and a brave officer who participated in numerous successful operations. In November- December 1992 we found him preparing and struggling with Military law paper in Part D examinations. He was forced to study with the commanding officer for ten days and he cleared his examination in the next attempt. In February 93 he was the first to give us successes from village Nohama and Chitargram. In both cases he was personally instrumental in digging out terrorists from hay stacks. RSK was also responsible for smooth conduct of Amaranth Yatra in 1993. He was positioned at the shrine alongwith Hardy commanding Delta company. There were no casualties, no mishaps or any other problem faced by the public. A total of 130000 people visited the shrine. We were visited by the Honourable Governor who complimented the battalion for the good job. A fair degree of successful conduct of the 'Yatra' was due to the efforts of Delta company under RSK Nair. Married to Ajishree Thampy, the couple have two daughters. The elder Nandini is pursuing her engineering in electronics and communication in Trivandrum and the younger Vaishnavi is in Xth standard.

Major (later Colonel) Mahendra Jogdand, Sena Medal, was the brave 'Bravo company commander who led his company with personal example of dynamism and competence. With numerous results to his credit, he was awarded Sena Medal for gallantry in active operations. He led his Gurkha company through chest deep icy cold waters of Vishwa river in April 1993 and surprised five terrorists who were immediately neutralized. In early September 1994 he was again instrumental in neutralizing four foreign terrorists in a village Yadir near Panchgam and recovery of five weapons. He took premature retirement in January 2009 and has settled down in Belgaum in Karnatka. He is working in Tata Motars in Dharwal. Married to Rashmi, they have two daughters, while Prithvi is studying Architecture the younger Tanya is preparing for medicine.

Major Avtar Singh, Sena Medal, was a short commissioned officer who joined us in Sri Lanka. A very daring and a brave officer, Avtar performed creditably well during operations in the valley. In a daring operation in Haft chinar in August 1992 he responded to militant fire by immediately jumping over the boundary wall and chasing them. His valiant efforts resulted in recovery of two A K Rifles. He was aptly awarded Sena Medal for this gallant action. He left service in March 1993, but later joined a territorial unit to once again return to J&K. He married in to a Kashmiri family and had three children. The family shifted to USA where in a fit of rage the gallant officer wiped out his family in March 2013.

Major (now Lt Colonel) Paramjot Singh Virk, another brave and competent officer, Paramjot was with the unit through out our tenure in the valley except for a short period that he was admitted in the hospital consequent to his accidental fire on 6 July 1993 in a village near Kulgam. He volunteered to rejoin the unit after he was discharged from the Command hospital, very well knowing that he could have gone to any peace station. The Military Secretary at Army Headquarters, is believed to have remarked that a special endorsement be made in his dossier for displaying extraordinary devotion and dedication to service. He continued to work hard, passed 'Staff Course' examination and is today posted in a Command headquarters. Married to Narinder from Bikaner they have a daughter Sirjana (Jagmag) who is studying in Xth standard.

Captain (now Colonel) Lakhbinder Singh Lidder, Sena Medal affectionatingly called 'Driver' was our Adjutant for most of our stay in the valley. An extremely brave, tough, bold and a mature officer, it was an honour to have him as part of our team. He only needed a brief indication and he would not only make a plan, but coordinate all aspects of movement and deployment with the Brigade Headquarters as also with the neighboring units. We owe a number of successes to him. It was he who spearheaded the Waltityang operation of 5 May 93. He initially caught the two terrorists, interrogated them and suggested the immediate launch of operation, which was done resulting in tremendous success. Our small team operations of 2 May, 9 May and to Wular lake in August 1993 were all attributed to him. On 8 February 1994, he was instrumental in recovering eight weapons from a terrorist. On 26 February and 1 March 1994 he was once again involved in eliminating foreign terrorists in Lariyar and Dadsura in Tral. In July 1994 he was instrumental in recovering 17 weapons from Srinagar. Throughout this tenure he was responsible for mature handling of our operations, management and administration of the unit. An extremely brave officer he would always insist in walking ahead of the CO. He was recommended for numerous awards and was awarded with a Sena Medal and two commendation cards. He has done extremely well in service, commanded the same unit, attended the 'Higher Command' course and after doing a stint in Delhi he has been posted as Defense Attaché to a mission abroad. Married to Geetika they have a daughter Aashna studying in 6th standard.

Captain (now Colonel) Hardeep Singh Sohi, Shaurya Chakra, Sena Medal, another competent officer served with the unit during its complete tenure in the valley. A very brave and a daring officer could be relied for any difficult task. As 'Intelligence Officer' and later as a company commander he had performed extremely well. Fondly remembers his chase in Waltityang on 5 May 93 alongwith the CO when they successfully surrounded two terrorists. His performance in Kaitson operation on 15 July 93 and in Turkpura encounter five days later was remarkable. Two months later in operation Alpine Noose he again performed extremely well. In that operation we eliminated a group of 24 terrorists. On that day there were very good chances of suffering causalities and Hardy had to be cautioned to crawl and close up with the terrorists which he dutifully did and the results were there for every one to see. In our last operation in the valley in Tral in April 1995 our friend Hardy was critically injured after neutralizing three militants. He was awarded Shaurya Chakra, Sena medal and a commendation card by Chief Of Army Staff for various operations conducted by him. Having been injured in operations Hardy shifted to 'Army Ordnance Corps' and has successfully commanded an Ordnance depot. He has also attended the prestigious Higher Command course. Married to Jasleen the couple have two sons. The elder Gulmehar is joining NSCIT Delhi for engineering and the younger Fateh is studying in Xth standard in Delhi.

Captain (now Lieutenant Colonel) Gulshan Chadha, an intelligent, brave, cheerful and a jovial officer. He was with the unit throughout our tenure. He underwent the rigours of the tough tenure with us and participated and led numerous small team operations displaying conspicuous bravery and gallantry of a very high order. He also assisted us in planning and coordinating operations whenever the permanent Adjutant was away. He participated in all major operations including one in Palno Panditpura in September 1994 where he got injured. The brave man that he is, kept his spirits up despite the acute pain that he had. During his evacuation the bad roads to Prisal and Arwini though increased his pain but the bullet fell out of his lower abdomen and helped him recover early. A very determined and brave officer he was always ready to launch himself in to any difficult task. He has continued to do well in service, learning the Chinese language and then taking up his favorite hobby of mountaineering as a full time profession. He is presently posted as Commandant of a mountaineering institution being set up by the Government of Arunachal Pradesh at Dirang Dzong near Bomdila. Married to Aradhana they have a son Himal studying in the Xth standard.

2/Lt (Now Col) Vinay Shahi, Sena Medal, joined the unit in January 1993. A very brave, daring and a committed officer Vinay showed his mettle in numerous operations in the valley. Countless successes alongwith Lakhbinder, Hardeep and Ashish. Vinay led our small team operations very willingly without fear of injury or loss of life. Some of the spectacular successes in which he particularly contributed were Operation Alpine Noose in which he neutralized three terrorists, operation Harigram, in Kulgam tehsil on 26 June 1994, resulted in elimination of a dreaded terrorist code Paley Khan, participated in operation in Srinagar on 16 July resulting in recovery of large number of weapons and finally spearheaded the operation in Bolus on 31 December 1994. In this operation while he neutralized the first terrorist, he was injured in a grenade attack that took away his eyesight from right eye. A robust and a strong man he has continued to perform well and he is a colonel now. Married to Ruby a young girl from valley they have a son and a daughter. The son Veer Vikram is studying in X standard and the daughter Vaibhavi is studying in 4th standard.

2/Lieutenant (now Colonel) Maheshwar Singh Andotra joined the unit in September 1993 just after we shifted to Manasbal. A smart, young, bold and energetic officer who actively participated in numerous operations alongwith his Delta Company. He saw action in Bandipur and in areas around including the one in October 1993 in which we eliminated 24 terrorists. He led a number of small team operations very successfully including the one in Palno Panditpura and in Operation Balsu on 31 December 1994. In this operation he was tasked to evacuate Vinay Shahi in a civil bus to Qaimuh and from there to Khanabal and then to Srinagar. That evening he returned back quickly to Balsu to participate in the continuing operation. By his sheer grit and determination he contributed to the success of the operation the next day in the afternoon. Maheshwar has continued to perform well in service. He qualified for the prestigious Defense Services Staff College course commanded the BODYGUARD battalion in high altitude operational sector of J&K. He attended the Air Higher Command course at Secunderabad and has been retained there as an instructor. Married to Namrata, they have two children a daughter and son. The elder Sonakshi is studying in 8 standard and Shivansh in 2 standard in Secunderabad.

Captain Amit Chatterjee, Sena Medal was the RMO of the unit. He was extremely competent, polite, understanding and prompt in administering medical aid to the troops as also to the civilians. He operated in the unit as a full member of the team. When required he would officiate as Adjutant and also as a company commander as and when some officer was not available. Always willing to accept additional responsibilities Amit with his qualities of compassion and care won hearts of the troops and of the public around. Sometimes he was also able to gather details of our friends (the terrorists). Awarded Sena Medal for bravery and dedication to service. He was a good check on all of us particularly while interrogating the terrorists; he would ensure safety and well being of all inmates. Amit is happily married and has settled down in Bangalore.

Captain (now Colonel) C M Singh, VSM, was our second RMO who did six months tenure with us from May 1993 till November that year. He came from Saichin to relieve Amit during this period. Professionally he was an excellent replacement. Physically tough he had tremendous compassion for all patients. During operations he would attend to looking after civilians too. Like Amit he would willingly carry out all duties of a regimental officer as well as of RMO. He would willingly officiate as adjutant and company commander when ever required. Having joined us on our return from Tral on 13 May 93 after a successful operation, he was fully acclimatized to participate in numerous operations. His performance in Operation Kaitson (15 July), Turakpura (20 July), Alpine Noose (6 Oct), Hazratbal (15 October to 15 November) and thereafter in Sopur (27 November) was commendable. He was also involved in neutralization of terrorists in operation Kaitson where he volunteered to operate with Hardy. He was recommended for a gallantry award like Amit however he did not get one there. Later in service he has been awarded with a VSM by the President of India. During our brief stint in the Holy shrine of Amaranth, he was responsible for providing medical aid to a large number of civilians which was duly commended upon by the Honourable Governor of Jammu and Kashmir. CM is happily married to Mrinalni, a trained graduate teacher by profession, the couple have a daughter Priya who is studying in Class VIII in Delhi. He is posted in Base Hospital in Delhi as an orthopedic surgeon where he operates six day a week to provide relief to large number of personnel and their families. His dedication and exemplary service brings him large number of patients which he ungrudgingly attends to, day after day.

Lieutenant (now Lieutenant Colonel) Q R Haidry joined the advance party of the unit in first week of April 1992 while it was located in old airfield. A young, sincere and a hardworking officer, Haidry soon got in to the grid of anti militant operations. Alongwith Major Paramjot, Gulshan and Lawand he operated with 15 GARHWAL RIFLES, the unit that we were relieving in and around Srinagar, On arrival of the unit he participated in all operations under Delta company in Pulwama district including the one in Pampore in August 1992 in which a famous terrorist Mushtaq Ahmed Latram was apprehended. This terrorist was involved in exchange of militants during the Kandhar crisis in 1998. Haidry had the misfortune of coming under two improvised explosives devices on 2 August 1992. The first one was in Pulwama market and the second near Rambhag Bridge in Srinagar. God was kind and he escaped unhurt from both these attacks. Haidry moved out in September that year. He has continued to do well in service. He is presently posted in NCC Group Headquarters in Hyderabad as training officer. Married to Rizwana, they have two daughters. The elder, Nirofer is in second year of graduation, she is also trying her hand on modelling. The younger Rukhsar is in 11 class.

2/Lieutenant (now Colonel) Lawand joined the unit in Lucknow in March 1992 and moved with the Battalion to Srinagar on induction to the valley. He stayed in the unit till September that year. During this period he participated in all operations particularly in Pulwama district where we had good successes. He was also assigned for road opening tasks on the Leh axis, a task that he performed creditably well. The leh axis remained incident free in our area of responsibility during that period. Married to Aarti, they have two daughters, while the elder one is in college, the younger Gesna is studying in class 10.

Lt P C Nayak was an officer from Army Ordnance Corps who joined us in September 1992 while we were at Haft Chinar. He did a short tenure for six months in the unit. A very sincere and a competent officer who understood the aspects of fighting militancy very well. He participated in numerous operations in the valley and contributed to the overall success of the unit particularly during the first two months of 1993 when we were concentrating on operations in Srinagar and Pulwama districts. He is presently posted in NCC in Cuttock, Orissa. Married to Nibedita, they have two sons, the elder Anurag is studying in IX and the younger Anupam is studying in VIII standard.

2/Lt (now Colonel) Ashish Maini joined us in Srinagar in December 1992 on attachment for one year. Throughout 1993 Ashish led numerous successful operations against the terrorists. He was always ready to accept any challenge that was faced by us. Always volunteered to join operations without fear for his own safety and welfare. An extremely brave and a daring officer he participated in number of successful operations. His contribution in a day light raid on a terrorist hideout in Waltiyang on 5 May and later in Sopur on 27 November was commendable. While in Waltityang we neutralized five terrorists, in Sopur there were seven. In this operation Ashish insisted on leading the CO QRT and walking ahead of the CO, after Lakhbinder got injured. Ashish performed duties of Adjutant very successfully. He was aptly awarded a Commendation Card by the COAS for bravery and distinguished service. He has also continued to perform extremely well in service. He has commanded an ASC Battalion in an Infantry Division and the 'Army Headquarters Transport Company' in Delhi very successfully. Happily married to Ruchi a para ordinance officer they have one daughter Varija studying in 8 standard.

2/Lt (now Lieutenant Colonel) Ashutosh Tripathi, an EME officer joined us in March 1993. A young officer with tremendous energy and will power, he will be long remembered for apprehending Sheikh Abdul Aziz, the 'Supreme Commander' of Al Jihad and 'Father of Militancy in J & K'. The Sheikh was apprehended in Village Nilura on 21 May 1993 alongwith ten of his bodyguards. The Sheikh when confronted Ashutosh told the latter that he was a big commander. Ashutosh could not comprehend his status and conveyed the same to the second in command. Little later Ashutosh realized the implication, when the entire valley was shut down for three days. He was undoubtedly a big catch, the credit for which goes to Ashutoash.

Lieutenant (now Colonel) Atul Apte joined us in January 1993 for his attachment of six months. An intelligent, hard working and a very spirited officer from corps of EME, Atul participated in numerous operations during that period. An effective junior leader he led many small team operations in Pulwama and Prisal areas. He contributed to our numerous successes particularly in our initial move and settling down in Prisal. Atul has also continued to perform well in service. He commanded an infantry division EME battalion in Jammu and Kashmir. He is now posted as General Manager Works in a base workshop. Married to Priya. The couple has a son Akshay studying in class VII.

2/Lieutenant (now Colonel) R R Tiwari joined us in December 1993 on attachment for one year, affectionately called 'junior' since we had one senior Tiwari in the unit. Junior performed extremely well. A brave and a daring officer who efficiently led numerous patrols against the terrorists. His contribution though short but was commendable. He has continued to perform extremely well in service. Already a Colonel who has successfully commanded an ASC battalion in a mountain division. Happily married to Anita, they have two children; while the elder Divya, is studying in 12, the younger Divanshu is studying in 10 standard respectively.

Lieutenant Abhay Awasthi a short commissioned officer from OTA Chennai joined us in March 1994 and served with the unit for six months. He was posted to Bravo Company under Major Jogdand, under whose guidance he participated in numerous operations. A good natured officer who was always cheerful, brave, dynamic and contributed immensely to over all success of numerous operations undertaken by his company and the unit. He was posted out on completion of his tenure in September 1994. He has continued to do well in service. Presently posted in ASC Centre and College Bangalore as Training officer. Married to Shivani (who is a textile designer), the couple have two children. The elder Aditya (14) is studying in X standard and the younger Ananya (12) is in 7 class. Aditya is an excellent rider and is expected to do well in equestrian sports.

2/Lt (now Lieutenant Colonel) MS Tanwar (also called MST in short) joined us in June 1994 in Prisal. Commissioned in Army Ordnance Corps, he did two years attachment with BODYGUARD. A very sincere, hardworking and a dedicated officer he participated in numerous successful operations. He carries a mark of valley with him like seven other officers who were injured in operations. While moving out from Prisal early in the morning in a three ton vehicle, the left wheel of which drove over an improvised explosive device near Yaripura. MST had, a few seconds earlier shifted closer to the driver since there was no window pane in the vehicle. That's what saved us. Though thrown out of the vehicle the brave officer took the blast in stride and continued to serve the Battalion without any hesitation. Married to Monica Singh, a housewife, the couple have two children a daughter and a son who are studying in Delhi.

Epilogue

It has been nearly twenty years since we operated in the Jammu and Kashmir valley. Looking back, the tenure of the battalion in Jammu and Kashmir from April 1992 to April 1995 was remarkable by all standards. Militarily there were excellent results, over seven dozen awards from Chief of Army Staff and by the Army Commander. A Citation of the unit by the Chief of Army Staff and another by the Army Commander highlighted the performance of the unit during this period. The continuous flow of messages of appreciation from various senior officers from the regiment and commanders up the chain was another indicator of the results achieved on ground by the brave soldiers of the unit.

There was an appreciable change in the environment from the time when we entered the valley and when we left in April 1995. Over 350 militants were eliminated by the battalion. This was acknowledged by the GOC 8 Mountain Division. In August 1990 while moving up from Udhampur on way to posting to unit in Gulmarg, we experienced that there was no civil movement of vehicles moving towards.the Valley at all. No one appeared to planning a holiday or their honeymoon in Srinagar any more. For miles we could see only one green bus conveying us and a three ton vehicle carrying our baggage. It looked like moving in to war zone. By April 1995 the situation had changed considerably.

Though militancy had not finished but the number of militant actions had definitely reduced. The Valley was back in to the grip and under the Government control. So much so that the elections could be safely conducted the following year under the eyes of both the national and International media. Tourism had restarted; Amaranth Yatra (pilgrimage) had been conducted successfully every year. All educational institutions and hospitals were functioning normally and movement of apples, walnuts (fruit and furniture) as also of woollen carpets and shawls had all boosted the economy. During the last 20 years, the valley is no longer as fearful as it looked in 1992. Politically the state has undergone assembly elections three times. People have expressed their opinion most willingly with greater numbers every time they have gone through the electoral process. Many politicians have though retained their seats while a good number of them have been rejected because of their poor performance. It is the free expression of the people of the state which is noteworthy.

The improved security situation has helped economic redevelopment, setting up of new schools and colleges all over the state. Famous names such as DPS have opened branches in all parts of the state including Srinagar, leh and in Jammu. Many people feel that they have been left behind in comparison to the rest of the country in fields of urbanization and development and they are demanding for more. The mushrooming of motar vehicles, mobile phones, TVs and other gadgets are all indicative of increased development which is all due to improved security situation. It gives us tremendous satisfaction that we were once part of this process and had contributed in a small measure in helping the state machinery in regaining control.

APPENDICES

जनरल बी सी जोशी

General B C Joshi
PVSM, AVSM, ADC

सेना मुख्यालय
नई दिल्ली - ११००११
Army Headquarters
New Delhi - 110011

A/21429/Gen/AG/CW-2

29 Dec 93

My dear Col Soneja,

1. My heartiest congratulations to all ranks of your unit for their outstanding performance of ' OP RAKSHAK' during the period from May 92 to May 93, for which I am awarding your unit my Appreciation on 15 Jan 94 at Army Day Parade at Delhi.

2. This may please be conveyed to All Ranks of your unit at a specially convened Sainik Sammelan.

3. I am confident that your unit will continue to maintain this high standard of devotion to duty and selfless service to the Nation, in the days to come.

With fond regards

Yours sincerely

B C Joshi

Col AC Soneja
Commanding Officer
2 JAK RIF
C/O 56 APO

Operation Hazratbal Message from Chief of Army Staff

OP HAZRATBAL (.) extracts of msg from COAS to GOC-in-C Northern Comd reproduced as follows (.)

firstly (.) the professional and effective mgt of Army Ops vis-a-vis the Armd militants hiding inside the HAZRATBAL mosque made singular contribution to the surrender of militants (.) the Ops control and media interaction was handed with commendable skills (.) civil military coordination and cooperation was sustained effectively (.)

secondly (.) the ops have highlighted the maturity comma resilience and dedication of our Army in handling complicated military ops in the aid to civ auth (.) the adaptation to novel tactics was indeed commendable (.)

thirdly (.) my admiration and felicitations be conveyed to all ranks (.)

well done (.) you have done me comma the Army and the country proud (.)

fourthly (.) next few days are vital to see the Op through to its logical conclusion (.) I am sanguine you will enforce the agreed bottom line (.) for info

लेफ्टिनेंट जनरल एस पदमानाभन, वी एस एम
जनरल अफसर कमांडिंग
Lt Gen S Padmanabhan, VSM
General Officer Commanding

मुख्यालय १५ कोर
द्वारा ५६ ए पी ओ
Headquarters 15 Corps
C/o 56 A P O

11859/SP/2

18 Nov 93

My dear Colonel,

1. During the recently concluded ops at Hazratbal, Srinagar your Bn was dply to sanitise a large area around the Shrine and prevent any external militant gps or agitated public from interfering with the cordon.

2. The performance of your Bn in this role was magnificent. The success of the entire op was in no small measure due to the very eff manner in which your Bn, under your able ldrship, performed this very sensitive and onerous task.

3. I wish to convey to you and all rks of your very fine Bn my personal gratitude and very high appre for your magnificent performance in this op. Well done! Keep up the good wk!

17 Nov 93

With best regards,

Sainik Samachar

Yours sincerely,

Padmanabhan

Col AC Soneja
Commanding Officer
2 JAK RIF
C/O 56 APO

लेफ्टीनेंट जनरल जे एस ढिल्लों, युद्ध सेवा मेडल
जनरल अफसर कमांडिंग
Lt Gen J S Dhillon, YSM
General Officer Commanding

मुख्यालय १५ कोर
द्वारा ५६ ए पी ओ
Headquarters 15 Corps
C/o 56 A P O

1001/5/MS

16 Feb 96

Dear Sonuje,

1. I would like to convey my appreciation to your unit for being conferred with u/m awards on the occasion of **Army Day/Republic Day 1996:-**

(a)	Capt Vinay Shahi	- SM
(b)	Capt Anil Chatterjee	- SM
(c)	Sub BB Chand	- SM
(d)	Rfn Jaswinder Kumar	- SM
(e)	Rfn Polas Sherpa	- SM
(f)	Rfn Roshan Singh	- SM
(g)	Lt Col GC Katoch	- COAS Commendation Card
(h)	2Lt RR Tiwari	- - do -
(j)	Hav Deepak Shahi	- - do -
(k)	Hav Gyan Singh	- - do -
(l)	Hav JK Sahi	- - do -
(m)	Nk Arjun Singh	- - do -
(n)	Rfn Dev Raj	- - do -
(o)	Capt Hardeep Singh, SM	- GOC-in-C Commendation Card
(p)	Sub Babar Jung	- - do -
(q)	Hav Jaswant Singh	- - do -

(r)	Hav Dharmendra Singh	- GOC-in-C Commendation Card
(s)	Sub RS Thapa	- - do -
(t)	Nb/Sub OC Rana	- - do -
(u)	Nk Sunit Singh	- - do -
(v)	Nk Richpal Singh	- - do -
(w)	L/Nk Rajmohan	- - do -
(x)	L/Nk Kartar Nath	- - do -
(y)	Rfn SK Pradhan	- - do -
(z)	Rfn Chetan Singh	- - do -

2. I hope that your unit will keep up the good work and earn more laurels. **Well done. Keep it up.**

With best wishes

Yours sincerely

Col AC Soneja, VSM
CO
2 JAK RIF
C/O 56 APO

Lt Gen G L Bakshi
PVSM (Retd)
Tele 89-74853

No 6 (S U)
Sector 37, ARUN VIHAR
NOIDA (U P)-201303

30 Apr 95

My dear Avinash,

I have received all your BRO's since 09Mar 95 outlining the outstanding and exceptional achievements of the Bn under your very able, inspiring and dynamic leadership. **Indeed your BRO dated 20 Apr 95 which sums up your tenure in the valley is a document to be preserved as it lists an outstanding and unbelievable set of achievements possibly unparalleled in the history of any Bn or Regt. 53 awards and many more on the way in one tenure is an achievement of which atleast I cannot think of any parallel. I therefore send to you and all ranks of the Bn my heartiest congratulations. Well done and god bless you all.**

I also learnt of the last action fought on 13 Apr in which Hardeep had providential escape, thanks to bullet proof jacket he was wearing. My Heartiest Congrats to him, L/Nk Raj Mohan and all others.

I wish you all a very happy tenure as part of 36 Bde which I had the privilege to command in 1980-82. Do look us up when you come to Delhi.

With My warm regards to all Offrs and best wishes to all Ranks and families.

Yours Sincerely
Gurn.

Lt Gen G L Bakshi
PVSM (Retd)
Telo 81 -S/K 74853

No 6 (S U)
Sector 37, ARUN VIHAR
NOIDA (U P) - 201303

06 Jul 95

My dear Avinash,

Thank you very much for your DO letter No 27264/ACS/Pers dated 19 Jun 95.

Now that **you have relinquished the command of 'BODYGUARD' let me convey to you that not only have you done yourself proud but the entire Regiment is proud of the achievements of the 'BODYGUARD' under your dynamic and very able and inspiring leadership. Indeed all of us who have known you for a long time, expected you to do well as CO but in your superlative performance you have far exceeded our legitimate expectations. If ever one is required to give an example of what a good leader can achieve and do to an outfit, yours will be the most apt and befitting example. You have in one stroke created history for the 'BODYGUARD' from which not only will future generations of Regtlpers particularly officers draw inspiration but also find it exceedingly difficult to surpass, even equal your record.** Well done Avinash and May God be with you in the future. Regt has great hopes in you.

You every inch deserve your nomination and selection for the Higher Command. I wish you a very happy and a successful stay at Mhow with family.

I may be coming to Mhow to give a talk to the SC course. The date suggested to me by the Commandant is 14 October and I am likely to accept it. It will be a pleasure meeting you unless you all are on a tour. Suman joins me in sending our warm regards to you both.

Yours Sincerely
Guru

Col A C Soneja, VSM
On HC Course
HC Wing
The College of Combat
Mhow (MP)

1819 • 1951

BODY GUARD

1963

बटालियन के ग्रादेश

BATTALION ROUTINE ORDERS

द्वारा

BY

ORDERS OF

कर्नल ए सी सुनेजा, वी एस एम

COL A C SONEJA, VSM

कमान ग्रफसर

COMMANDING OFFICER

द्वितीय बटालियन जम्मू ग्रौर काश्मीर राईफल्स

2nd BATTALION THE JAMMU AND KASHMIR RIFLES

C/o 56 APO *SERIAL* 12/S/95 *DATE* 20 Apr 95

COMPLIMENTRY MESSAGE

1. This Part 1 order is being issued to commemorate the" **BODYGUARD**" **Bn's** successful tenure in the valley that commenced on 18 Apr 92 and is likely to terminate on 23 Apr 95. As we step across the Banihal tunnel it gives us all a tremendous satisfaction for our small contribution in bringing peace to the troubled valley.

2. As we leave the confines of the beautiful Kashmir valley we take pride in the fact that there are **358 militants less including 168 killed in 58 successful armed encounters with the ANE's. The Bn carried out 581 operations of which 192 were successful resulting in recovery of 247 weapons, besides a large qty of amn and explosives. One Supreme Commander, three Dist Cdrs and four Bn Cdrs of various militant outfits were eliminated by the brave boys.**

3 This tenure and performance of the "**BODYGUARD**" Bn in OP RAKSHAK(J&K) **will indeed be written in golden letters. The tenure has brought us a total of 53 awards so far. Many more will certainly follow.** The heroic efforts of the Bn were repeatedly lauded by various Cdrs. **A total of 44 complimentary messages were received which included 8 from COAS, 9 from GOC-in-C and 8 from GOC 15 Corps.** Amongst the other achievements the **unit earned the prestigious award of Unit Citation from the COAS on 15 Jan 94, a silver plaque for outstanding performance in J&K from HE The Governor of J&K on 13 Sep 94 and finally a Unit Appreciation from the GOC-in-C Northern Command on 29 Mar95.** We most sincerely thank' **DURGE MATA'** and all our serving and retd sr offrs and well wishers for their continued blessing, good wishes and guidance.

4. On this day we humbly remember the under/mentioned brave soldiers who made the supreme sacrifice in service to our Nation:

(a)	JC 185262A	Sub	Omkar Singh Manhas
(b)	13741349Y	Hav	Pyar Singh
(c)	13742820A	L/Hav	Nek Singh, SC
(d)	13742447L	Nk	Jagan Nath
(e)	13743718K	L/Nk	Naresh Kumar, SC
(f)	13748518X	Rfn	Joginder Kumar
(g)	13750862F	Rfn	Phula Sherpa
(h)	13751542Y	Rfn	Rajeshwar Singh, SC

It is the sacrifices of these brave soldiers as also of 8 Offrs, 5 JCO's, and 38 other ranks who were injured in various encounters and IED attacks that has brought this glory to the bn.

Let us pray to DURGE MATA to give us strength and perseverance to continue doing all tasks with similar zeal and fervour in yrs to come.

'JAI DURGE'

(A C Soneja)
Col
CO

Maj Gen S S Grewal, AVSM, SM, VSM
Colonel, The Jammu and Kashmir Rifles
Colonel The Ladakh Scouts

SCOUTS
LADAKH

HQ II Corps
C/o 56 APO

COR/C/G&C/58 06 Jun 95

My Dear Avinash.

1. On your having relinquished the comd of Body Guard, it gives me great pleasure to place on record my deep appreciation and commendation for all the good work that you have done during your tenure. It is my firm impression, that you have contributed a great deal to the well-being and professional advancement of the Bn and were held in very high esteem by your subordinates as also by your seniors in the fmn. Keeping this in view, I would like to convey my heartiest congratulations and I have no doubt that you would have left the Bn with a deep sense of satisfaction, having done your best.

2. I take this opportunity to wish you all success and best of luck in your new appt, future career and life.

With warm regards
Yours Sincerely
Sarabjit Singh

Col AC Soneja,VSM
Commanding Officer
2 JAK RIF
c/o 56 APO

Seen

Major General D B Shekatkar, VSM
General Officer Commanding

Headquarters
8 Mountain Division
C/o 56 APO

14765/DBS/1

8th Jun 95

My dear Soneja.

1. Thank you ever so much for your DO letter No 27264/ACS/Pers dt 19 Jun 95.

2. I was deeply impressed to receive the letter from you and am really proud of the achievements won by the Battalion under your stewardship.

3. I am sure with the tireless efforts, dedication to the service and above all the experience you gained will be very useful to your new establishment and I am confident you will contribute the maximum for the betterment of the Army as a whole.

4. I wish you a very happy, successful and prosperous life.

With warm Regards.

Yours sincerely,

Shekatkar

Col AC Soneja,VSM
College of Combat
HC Course
MHOW (MP)

मेजर जनरल आर एस मावी, ए वी एस एम, एस सी
कमांडर
Maj Gen R S Mavi, AVSM, SC
Commander

सीनियर कमान्ड विंग
कम्बाट कॉलेज
महू (म. प्र.) ४५३४४१
Senior Command Wing
The College of Combat
Mhow (M P) 453441

12637/RSM/ACR/FI/SC — 18 Oct 93

My dear Soneja,

1. It is indeed wonderful to learn about another astounding success achieved by 2 JAK RIF in its relentless offensive action against militants by eliminating 23 of them (nine foreigners) and recovery of a considerable number of weapons and ammunition. The action speaks volumes of your inspiring leadership and dedication of all ranks towards the National cause.

2. I pray that the blessing of Durge Mata be showered on the Bn for its continued success and glory in the challenges ahead during conduct of anti-insurgency operations.

Thanks for the DO letter.

With best wishes,

Yours sincerely
Mavi

Col AC Soneja
Commanding Officer
2nd Battalion
Jammu and Kashmir Rifles
C/O 56 APO

Lt Col O P Singh
Officer Commanding

1 Bengal Armoured Squadron NCC
NCC House, Fort William
Calcutta-700 021

25059/Pers

27 Jul 95

My Dear Col Sangja,

1 I am in receipt of your DO Letter no. 27264/ACS/Pers dated 19 Jun 95. Please accept our heartiest congratulations on completion of a very successful command tenure. I fully agree with you that ' BODY GUARD ' is second to none. The bn has all the ingradients required for an outstanding performer ; however it needed your grit, determination dedication and leadership to do what they did.

2 We, the people of ' Body Guard', are indebted to you, for having once again taken the ' BODY GUARD' lance to the heights, it so rightly deserves. The history would record the courrage and conviction with which you led the glorious march to widely acclaimed successes. My wife joins me in extending our heartiest congratulation to you on your excellent performance.

Wishing you all the best for your HC Course
Please convey our warm regards to Mrs Sangja
With regards and best wishes

Yours Sincerely

Col A C Sangja, V S M
Higher Command
Coursesr - 24
College of combat
M H O W (M.P.)

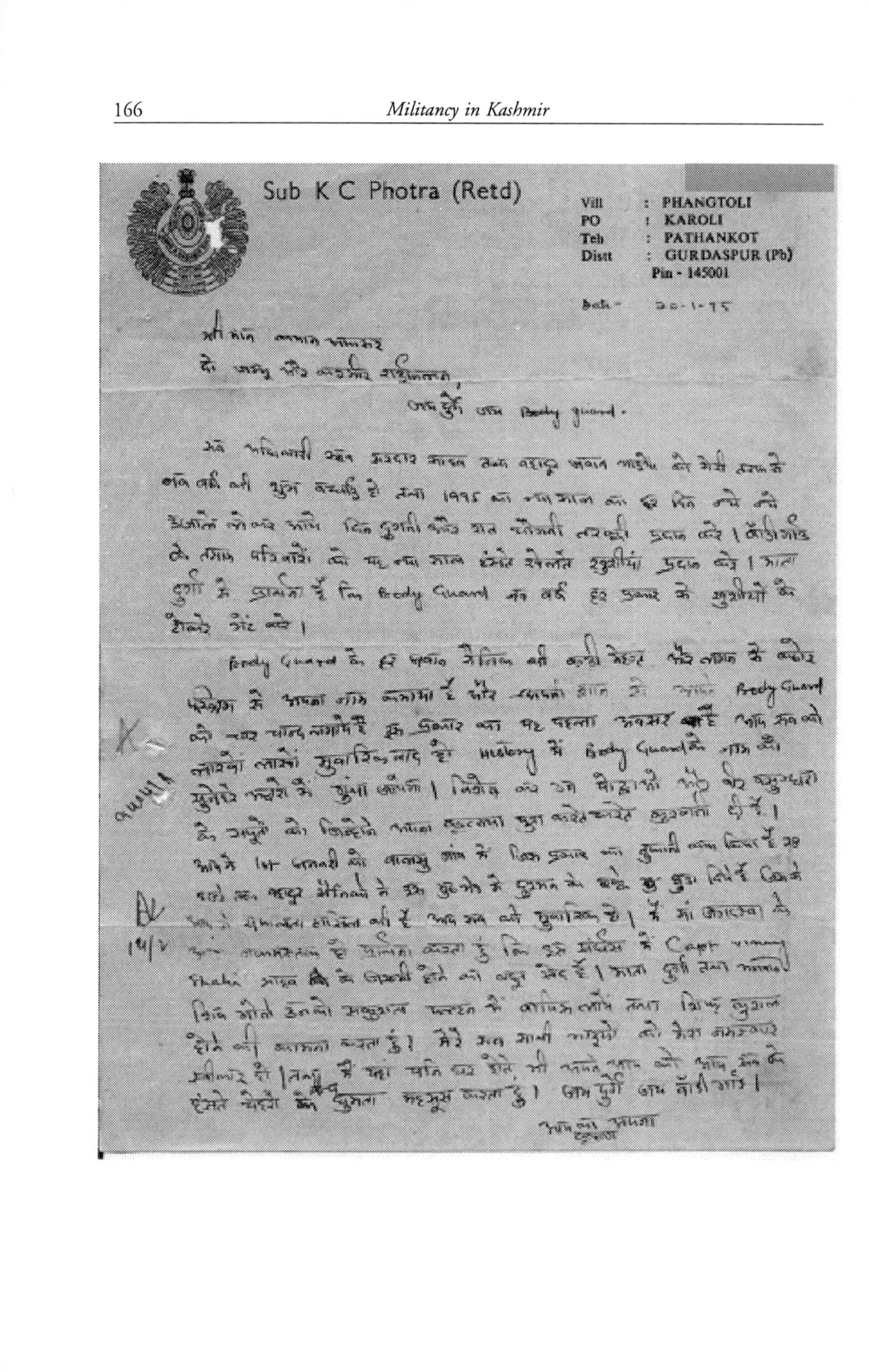

Sub K C Photra (Retd)

Vill : PHANGTOLI
PO : KAROLI
Teh : PATHANKOT
Distt : GURDASPUR (Pb)
Pin - 145001

Date - 20-1-95

The Shadow of a Horse by François Gautier

(names of officers changed due to reasons of security)

Midnight, Manasbal Lake, North-West Kashmir. The powerful diesels of the 20 army lorries roar away, piercing the perfect silence of the night. Aboard, 400 men of the 22nd Jammu and Kashmir Rifles, one of India's elite divisions, in full battle dress: helmets, an AK-47 rifle slung over the shoulder and two grenades tucked in the belt. Colonel Khanna, division commander, signals with his hand and the convoy starts ponderously into the night.

Earlier we had met Colonel Khanna's officers, young, bright men, whose world centres around a field tent, the walls of which are adorned with pictures of wanted militants, and tallies of wounded and killed Hizbollah Mujahedins, a true soldier's trophy. Over a glass of beer, Colonel Khanna had shown us a map of Kashmir and pointed to a village near Wular Lake, called Banyar. "This village, he said, is known to be a safe haven for militants, as it is on the route from Kupwara at the Pak border, to Sopore. It has the uniqueness of being surrounded by water. So we will have to take two boats with us to cross the river. We shall walk the whole night and by morning we will have surrounded the entire village."

Half an hour after, having started from the base, the Lorries stopped suddenly, all lights out. Silently the 400 men of the regiment climbed down and melted into the night. Then the lorries started again. "They will serve as a decoy for the militants' watchdogs, who seeing they are going in an opposite direction, will think that we are going to strike another village," whispered Khanna. It was a pitch-dark monsoon night. No lights, no torches, one could barely discern the man in front and sometimes soldiers would hold each other's shoulders not to get lost. The silence was total: not a murmur, not a sound of a rolling stone; only the hiss of the wind in the trees, carrying the smell of men to a faraway village, whose dogs started barking. But even their sounds slowly died away. Suddenly, a cantering horse, like a ghost appearing from nowhere, crossed us; and then it was gone, as in a dream.

At first, the going was smooth enough on a dirt road, but all of a sudden we had to slither down on all fours to reach the swamp, where one had now to walk on a high narrow causeway surrounded by water on both sides. It started raining and a frog, followed by another, then another, then a hundred, a thousand, began tearing the silence of the night with their "croaaroaaak". From time to time the man in front would suddenly stop and the others behind would bump into him: the soldiers carrying the heavy wooden boats were to be replaced by a new team. At 3.30 in the morning, the river had to be crossed to reach the village. The boats were lowered into the water without a ripple; and while exhausted men slept on the embankment, the tedious task of carrying a whole company in two boats went on smoothly. And as the first hint of a grey, dreary day, pointed at the horizon, the village of Banyar was totally surrounded. Lieutenant Tikku and a platoon of soldiers entered the village from its eastern side. "Militants are usually caught at daylight, he murmured, it is then that they start shooting. If we don't catch them at that moment, they go into hiding either in the houses or in the fields; and we have to flush them out." Shoulders hunched in the expectation of a grenade thrown from the first floor of a house, or the bullet of an unseen sniper, eyes darting right and left, fingers on the triggers of their AK-47s, the soldiers advanced on the village. It was a dreadful hamlet on the banks of the Jhelum River: dirty, unkempt, whose wooden and cement houses had an air of never having been finished. By 6 AM, not a soul had stirred from the shuttered houses, and it became clear that if the militants were there, they were not going to come out with guns blazing. An officer went to the mosque and asked on its loudspeakers that all men between 16 and 60 assemble in the school compound just outside the village.

Already soldiers had encircled the meadow where a little windowless house which served as school stood. Machine guns were posted; even a mortar was set up. Slowly the villagers started filing out of the village. The older men were put on the right where they sat stoically on their haunches; and the younger ones grouped on the left. After some time two men, whose faces were hooded by black cloth and their hand tied to a soldier, came in and were made to sit in the school, facing the glassless window. They were "cats" – militants who had been caught and who had agreed to inform on their brothers, in exchange for some future leniency. They were now at least 2,000 villagers in the meadow. On a signal from the Colonel, young villagers were made to form a file. First they were searched by a soldier, then one by one they were presented by another soldier to the cats. One of the informers seemed unwilling or maybe indifferent; but the other had extraordinary eyes, which were constantly darting, from the face of the soldier, to the villager. The villagers, some humble, others proud, others looking spitefully towards the informers, or a few eyes cast down in fear, filed past the cats. When the second informer would nod negatively the soldier would tap the shoulder of the villager, who relieved, would go back to sit on his haunches. But suddenly, as a mullah, well-dressed, apparently educated, looking boldly ahead, was brought forward, the cat raised his finger and whispered something in the ear of his watcher. The mullah was then led, protesting, to one corner and made to cover his face with his shawl. Four men were thus "recognized" by the second cat and kept apart.

Suddenly a shot was heard, followed by a burst of fire. Everybody rushed towards the place where the sound came from. There, in a field of mature maze, there was a path of crushed stalks, which led straight to two cowering militants, one of whom was wounded, surrounded by triumphant soldiers. Basir Ahmed Pare and Zakir Hussein had just crossed over, from Pakistan where they had gone for training and halted overnight in the village thinking they were safe. But when they realized that the army had surrounded the village, they hid in the field with their two Kalashnikov and four grenades. The weapons were recovered from them, with coupons which they sell to the villagers to extort money and the photo of their area commander. The men were then handed over to the military intelligence for what would probably be a long spell of rough interrogation.

Exhausted, after a whole night walk, plus a full day in the heat, we wearily started for the base. On the trip back, a riderless galloping horse (the same as in the night?) cast his shadow on our convoy. Was it the shadow of Kashmir?

—François Gautier

A Tribute to Late Lance Havildar Nek Singh, Shaurya Chakra

By Maj NK Bhatnagar
Published in Durjey, 1995

It was in August 1984, while attending the 'Junior Command' course I first heard the term 'FORCE MULTIPLIER' during the opening address of the course. As usual with me, the term went either over or through my head. I do not remember, I didn't bother, neither did I care, since I thought it was related to mechanized warfare. Eleven years later, once again in the College of Combat I heard this term. This time it did not fly past my head it was well understood and registered, not because I had joined a mechanized column but because I had seen a '**FORCE MULTIPLIER**' in my own outfit. This was not a tank or helicopter or a technological item, but a human being, in normal shape and size, and a brave soldier **Lance Havildar Nek Singh, SC of BODYGUARD Battalion.**

Born on 5 July 1960 in village Kahnal of District Doda, Nek Singh was enrolled on 8 May 1979. Next year he joined us at YOI Camp. A few days later in a company barakhana all of a sudden he caught the attention of all of us. Here he was a young boy who could sing and dance to the tune of Dogri, Nepali, Gujjari, Kumaoni and Kashmiri tunes. His pleasing personality, charming manners and dauntless courage soon endeared him to his comrades and seniors alike. He jumped into the mortar platoon within four years and soon became the best detachment commander capable of achieving miracles at the mortar end.

With the induction of the battalion in the Valley his other qualities came to the fore front. Being fluent in Gujjari and Kashmiri he volunteered for any hazardous mission at any time of the day and night. He soon became an inseparable part of CO's 'Quick Reaction Team'. Any operation, anywhere in the Valley, day or night, in uniform or civil dress, not withstanding the mode of transport, Nek Singh was the most willing individual to join. Imagine him raiding a militant hideout, dressed like a militant, located at two thousand feet high feature near Waltiyung in broad day light, and bringing laurels to the unit. The feat brought him a Shaurya Chakra and appreciations form GOC-in-C. Many more places like Arwani, Yaripora, Bandipora, Sopur, Bunyari, Kaimuh, Khudweni remind us of his indomitable spirit bravery and courage, His offensive spirit and courage brought him two more GOC-in-C's Commendation Cards.

On 7 August 1994, while on a 'Seek Encounter Patrol' with one officer and four other personnel, once again he got involved in a severe fire fight with the militants in village Rahpura, near Turk Tashlu, tehsil Kulgam, and district Anantnag. Displaying unparalleled courage and bravery, Nek Singh, SC shot two militants dead, pushed Lieutenant Vinay Shahi aside from the line of fire and got seriously injured. Cheerful that he was, he bravely told his comrades not to get unduly perturbed about himself. With forced evacuation to 92 Base Hospital on 7 Aug 94 by helicopter our brave Nek Singh the FORCE MULTIPLIER underwent yet another battle that was to last nine days and eight nights. All of us in the Unit stood still, with a prayer on our lips requesting God Almighty to allow him to join our folds once again, Alas that was not to be. Our **FORCE MULTIPLIER** - the brave soldier left us at 1400 hours on 15 Aug 1994. He was awarded Kirti Chakra (Posthumous) for the daring feat on 7 Aug 1994. Next morning wrapped in the National Tricolor he quietly marched out of the Valley to the extended hands of the Tenacious Tenth who gave him a befitting farewell at Udhampur.

Today six months later the BODYGUARD team misses him dearly, without our **FORCE MULTIPLIER**, we feel greatly handicapped. We wish 'YOU' were here with us today to bid farewell to the beautiful Valley where we lived and fought to bring peace to the hapless population and where we soldiered to keep our great country together. Though physically separated, you will always remain with us, in the mind of every member of the BODYGUARD family. We salute you and your brave wife and children. May God bless them with strength to bear this loss bravely.

Details of Armed Encounters

Ser No	Date	Place	Terrorist Killed	Recoveries	
1	30 May 92	Goripura	-	Rif AK-56	06
				Mag AK-56	06
				Amn AK-56	150
2	25 Jun 92	Bunagund	01	Rif AK-56	01
				Mag AK-56	02
				Amn AK-56	150
3	7 Jul 92	Aloochi Bagh	-	Rif AK-56	02
				Mag AK-56	02
				Amn AK-56	50
4.	2 Feb 93	Nanar	01	Rif AK-56	01
				Mag AK-56	03
				Amn AK-56	68
				Gren	01
5.	2 April 93	Kharbrara	01	Rifle AK-56	01
				Mag AK-56	01
				Amn AK-56	24
6.	4 April 93	Chhitarpura	01 and appre-04	Rif AK 56	05
				Mag AK 56	09
				Amn AK 56	207
7.	16 April 93	Kujar	01	Rif AK 56	01
				Mag AK 56	01
				Amn AK 56	02
8.	2 May 93	Mohandpur	01	Rif AK 56	01
				Mag AK 56	01
				Amn AK 56	17

9.	5 May 93	Waltiyung	05	Rif AK 56	06
				Mag AK 56	16
				Amn AK 56	440
				Gren	03
10.	9 May 93	Matalhama	01	Rif AK 56	01
				Mag AK 56	03
				Amn AK 56	43
				Gren	01
11.	12 May 93	Brintal (Tral)	02	Rif AK 56	02
				Mag AK 56	05
				Amn AK 56	125
				Gren	01
12.	21 May 93	Nilur	Appre hended-11	Rif AK 56	05
				Mag AK 56	11
				Amn AK 56	290
				Pistol	03
				Mag Pistol	02
				Amn Pistol	16
				Gren	01
13.	13-14 Jun 93	Damal Hanzioura	02	Rif AK 56	01
				Mag AK 56	02
				Amn AK 56	20
				Gren	01
14.	4 Jul 93	Yaripura	02	Rif AK 56	01
				Mag AK 56	04
				Amn AK 56	113
15.	15 Jul 93	Belipura /Kiatsan	09	Rif AK 56	05
				Mag AK 56	16
				Amn AK 56	279
16.	20 Jul 93	Turakpura	05	Rif AK 56	02
				Mag AK 56	07
				Amn AK 56	175
				Pistol	02
				Mag	02
				Amn	09
				Amn UMG	23
				Gren	03

17.	20 Aug 93	Banyari	01	Rif AK 56	01
				Mag AK 56	04
				Amn AK 56	104
18.	15 Sep 93	Dogipura	01	Rif AK 56	01
				Mag AK 56	04
				Amn AK 56	22
				12 Bore Gren	01
19.	29 Sep 93	Kondabal	04	Rif AK 56	03
				Mag AK 56	10
				Amn AK 56	195
				RS	01
20.	6 Oct 93	Malangam	23	UMG	01
				Mag UMG	01
				Amn UMG	86
				GPMG	01
				Mag GPMG	01
				Amn GPMG	14
				RPG 7V	01
				Rif AK 56	06
				Mag AK 56	14
				Amn AK 56	302
				Pistol	01
				Mag pistol	01
				Amn pistol	12
				Binocular	01
				RS	01
				Gren	08
21.	12 Oct 93	Chittibande	01	Rif AK 56	01
				Mag AK 56	03
				Amn AK 56-	120
				RS	01
22.	27 Nov 93	Sopur	07	Rif AK 56	05
				Mag AK 56	25
				Amn AK 56	747
20.	6 Jan 94	Tahab	01	Rif AK 56	01
				Mag AK 56	04
				Amn AK 56	50

21.	15 Jan 94	Tankipura	01	Rif AK 56	01
				Mag AK 56	03
				Amn AK 56	30
				Gren	01
22.	1 Feb 94	Hattipura/Dachau	03	Rif AK 56	01
				Mag AK 56	
				Amn AK 56	59
				Gren	01
23.	6 Feb 94	Frisal	01	Rif AK 56	01
				Mag AK 56	02
				Amn AK 56	35
24.	26 Feb 94	Lariyar	04	Rif AK 56	04
				Mag AK 56	06
				Amn AK 56	54
				Pistol	01
				Mag pistol	02
				Amn pistol	08
				Gren	03
25.	4 Mar 94	Naobal	02	Rif AK 56	01
				Mag AK 56	02
				Amn AK 56	51
				Gren	01
26.	9 Mar 94	Nulai/Pushwari/ Turkwangam	02	Rif AK 56	02
				Mag AK 56	03
				Amn AK 56	34
				Gren	01
27.	10 Mar 94	Batnur	01	Rif AK 56	01
				Mag AK 56	02
				Amn AK 56	39
				Gren	01
28.	28 Mar 94	Manchhu	02	Rif AK 56	02
				Mag AK 56	04
				Amn AK 56	78
				Gren	01

29.	31 Mar 94	Tarigam Deosar	01	Pistol	01
				Mag pistol	01
				Amn pistol	11
30.	4 April 94	Derapuraa	01	Rif AK 56	01
				Mag AK 56	02
				Amn AK 56	51
31.	30 April 94	Kathpura	02	Rif AK 56	02
				Mag AK 56	03
				Amn AK 56	46
				RS	01
32.	7 May 94	Batpura	01	Rif AK 56	01
				Mag AK 56	03
				Amn AK 56	71
33.	10 May 94	Kadir	01	Rif AK 56	01
				Mag AK 56	02
				Amn AK 56	49
34.	20 May 94	Chitragam	04	Pistol	01
				Mag pistol	02
				Amn pistol	12
				Gren	01
35.	28 May 94	Kaimuh	01	Rif AK 56	01
				Mag AK 56	03
				Amn AK 56	50
				Mag Pistol	01
				Amn Pistol	05
36.	11 Jun 94	Panyoh	04	Rif AK 56	04
				Mag AK 56	12
				Amn AK 56	32
37.	20 Jun 94	Kaimuh	01	Rif AK 56	01
				Mag AK 56	02
				Amn AK 56	33
38.	26 Jun 94	Hadigam	02	Rif AK 56	02
				Mag AK 56	06
				Amn AK 56	79
39.	9 Jul 94	Petha Reduna	01	Rif AK 56	01
				Mag AK 56	03
				Amn AK 56	04

40.	10 Jul 94	Kokargund	01	Rif AK 56 Mag AK 56 Amn AK 56	01 02 43
41.	19 Jul 94	Kadikadal	01	Rif AK 56 Mag AK 56 Amn AK 56	01 03 62
42.	21 Jul 94	Kharbrara/ Bogund	02	Rif AK 56 Mag AK 56 Amn AK 56	02 04 33
43.	7 Aug 94	Rahpura	02	Rif AK 56 Mag AK 56 Amn AK 56 Gren	01 01 05 01
44.	12 Aug 94	Bhan	01	Rif AK 56 Mag AK 56 Amn AK 56	01 03 30
45.	18 Aug 94	Kaimuh	04	Rif AK 56 Mag AK 56 Amn AK 56 RS	02 04 57 01
46.	25 Aug 94	Naupura	01	Rif AK 56 Mag AK 56 Amn AK 56 Gren	01 04 40 01
47.	3 Sep 94	Yadir	04	Rif AK 56 Mag AK 56 Amn AK 56 Pistol Mag Pistol Amn Pistol	03 11 330 02 04 95
48.	4 Sep 94	Katarsu	01	Rif AK 56 Mag AK 56 Amn AK 56	01 02 31
49.	7 Sep 94	Palno Panditpura	03	Rif AK 56 Mag AK 56 Amn AK 56	03 07 51

50.	19 Sep 94	Khelangund	01	Rif AK 56 Mag AK 56 Amn AK 56	01 02 01
51.	1 Oct 94	Tuli Nawpura	01	Rif AK 56 Mag AK 56 Amn AK 56 Gren	01 03 63 02
52.	29 Oct 94	Matibug	02	Rif AK 56 Mag AK 56	02 04
53.	30 Nov 94	Buchru	02	Rif AK 56 Mag AK 56 Amn AK 56	02 07 165
54.	14 Dec 94	Brazul Jagir	01	Rif AK 56 Mag AK 56 Amn AK 56	01 02 33
55.	31 Dec 94/ 1 Jan 95	Bolus	03	Rif AK 56 Mag AK 56 Amn AK 56	02 06 65
56.	8 Mar 95	Wagad	01	Rif AK 56 Mag AK 56 Amn AK 56 Pistol Mag Pistol Amn Pistol Gren	01 05 65 01 02 20 01
57.	10 Mar 95	Turki Tachlu	01	Rif AK 56 Mag AK 56 Amn AK 56	01 3 145
58.	13 April 1995	Nargistan	03	Rif AK 56	03

Casualities in 'OP Rakshak' (J&K) (1992-95)

Ser No	Army No	Rank	Name	Date of Cas	Remarks
MARTYRS					
1.	JC-185262A	Sub	Omkar Singh Manhas	11 Sep 94	
2.	13741349Y	Hav	Pyar Singh	7 Sep 94	
3.	13742820A	Hav	Nek Singh, SC	7 Aug 94 (15 Aug 94)	
4.	13742447L	Nk	Jagan Nath	23 Nov 94	
5.	13743718X	L/Nk	Naresh Kumar, SC	15 Jul 93	
6.	13748518K	Rfn	Joginder Kumar	07 Sep 94	
7.	13750862F	Rfn	Phula Sherpa	7 Sep 94	
8.	13751542Y	Rfn	Rajeshwar Singh, SC	12 May 93	
WOUNDED					
1.	IC-33802K	Maj	HS Gill	4 Jul 93	
2.	IC-49341P	Maj	Paramjot Singh	6 Jul 93	
3.	IC-49905M	Maj	Lakhbinder Singh, SM	27 Nov 93	
4.	IC-52384P	2Lt	RR Tiwari	9 Jul 94	
5.	JC-169265K	Sub	Faizu Ram	20 Jun 94	
6.	JC-176420H	Sub	Siddha Bahadur Mall	9 Jul 94	
7.	JC-224305H	Nb/ Sub	Kartar Singh	15 Jul 93	
8.	JC-578192X	Nb/ Sub	Puran Bahadur Shresht	9 Jul 94	
9.	13738090H	Hav	Sham Lal	2 May 93	
10.	13738962A	Hav	Krishan Kumar	20 Jun 94	
11.	13746853H	Nk	Budhi Bahadur	27 Nov 93 & 26 Jun 94	
12.	13742393P	Nk	Pawan Kumar	26 Feb 94	
13.	13743081L	Nk	Subash Singh	7 Aug 94	
14.	13741673W	Nk	Suneet Singh	21 Jul 94	
15.	13747309N	Nk	Arvind Kumar Gurung	26 Aug 94	
16.	13742450L	L/Nk	Manohar Lal	1 Aug 92	
17.	13747675X	L/Nk	Mekh Bahadur Gurung	1 Aug 92	

Ser No	Army No	Rank	Name	Date of Cas	Remarks
18.	13748317Y	L/Nk	Jai Bahadur Gurung	1 Aug 92	
19.	13742387F	L/Nk	Piar Singh	20 Nov 92	
20.	13747243H	L/Nk	Shiv Kumar	13 Apr 94	
21.	13743628H	L/Nk	Parma Nand	13 Jul 94	
22.	13748363L	L/Nk	Dal Bahadur	26 Aug 94	
23.	13748537H	Rfn	Koshal Kumar	2 May 93	
24.	13750620Y	Rfn	Kumar Thapa	2 May 93	
25.	13754447W	Rfn	Bimal Bharti	2 May 93	
26.	13751564X	Rfn	Jagdish Raj	2 May 93	
27.	13745984F	Rfn	Naresh Kumar Thapa	5 May 93	
28.	13748518X	Rfn	Joginder Kumar	15 Jul 93	
29.	13752223Y	Rfn	Ghan Shyam	15 Jul 93	
30.	13751522L	Rfn	Gorakh Singh	20 Jun 94	
31.	13747860L	Rfn	Krishan Singh	20 Jun 94	
32.	13748511N	Rfn	Ashok Kumar	20 Jun 94	
33.	13752218N	Rfn	Nand Lal	20 Jun 94	
34.	13751276L	Rfn	Dev Raj Gurung	9 Jul 94	
35.	13751660M	Rfn	Nar Bahadur	9 Jul 94	
36.	13752018X	Rfn	Roshan Singh	9 Jul 94	
37.	13750715Y	Rfn	Jit Bahadur Gurung	21 Jul 94	
38.	13750468W	Rfn	Harka Bahadur Thapa	26 Aug 94	
39.	13751027M	Rfn	Kharak Bahadur Gurung	7 Sep 94	
40.	JC-185262A	Sub	Omkar Singh Manhas	7 Sep 94	
41.	3743352P	Hav	Prem Singh	7 Sep 94	
42.	IC-52977F	2Lt	MS Tanwar	14 Nov 94	
43.	13740179N	Hav	Vijay Kumar	14 Nov 94	
44.	13750388Y	Hav	Hans Raj	23 Nov 94	
45.	13742446H	Nk	Ratan Singh	23 Nov 94	
46.	13751578X	Rfn Wtr	Dudekula Kasim	23 Dec 94	
47.	IC-51808B	Lt	Vinay Shahi	31 Dec 94	
48.	13750991F	Rfn	Dal Bahadur Gurung	3 Apr 95	
49.	IC-50927X	Capt	Hardeep Singh, SM	13 Apr 95	
50.	13743350M	L/Nk	Raj Mohan	13 Apr 95	
51.	SS-35181 P	Capt	Gulshan Chadha	7 Sep 94	
BATTLE ACCIDENT					
52.	JC-578291A	Nb Sub	Parkash Chand	28 Sep 94	

Gallantry Awards Earned by BODYGUARD Battalion

The gallantry displayed by all ranks in the unit was undoubtedly remarkable. The results and the awards earned by the unit during this period was one of the best by any unit in the entire period of insurgency in the valley. It had definitely achieved the distinction of becoming one of the best battalions that have operated in the valley. Numerous signals and telegrams initiated by various headquarters and senior officers and commanders clearly show that the unit had done its task exceedingly well. Though the list of awardees contain only 86 names but many more deserved them too. We took these awards in the stride and repeatedly spoke to the men that their bravery was definitely well recognized. They were advised to leave the rest to the God Almighty. And as it turned out 12 years later the unit was nominated to go abroad on a UN mission to Congo.

Details of awards earned by the unit both pre and after independence are given in the succeeding pages. The list also contains names of all ranks awarded during the tenure of the unit in the valley.

PRE INDEPENDENCE

Serial No	*Award*	*Year*	*Operation*	*Total*
1.	Victoria Cross	1891	Hunja Nagar	01
2.	IOM	1891	Hunja Nagar	01
3.	IOM Class II	1914-18	World War-1	06
4.	IOSM	1914-18	World War-1	05
5.	DSO			01
6.	IOM Class III			04
7.	CIE			02
8.	OBI			03
9.	Medagila-di-Bronze Valor Militareal (Italian)			01
10.	IMSM			09
11.	Mention In Dispatches			15
12.	Order of St Stanilas Class II with Sword (Russian)			01
13.	Order of St Gaerivede Guerre			01
14.	Order of St George (Russian Class IV)			02
15.	Coroix D Legion D Honour Chevalier			01
16.	Medalle Militar (French)			01
17.	OBE			01
18.	Good Service Cards			12
19.	Sena Medal			01

POST INDEPENDENCE

Serial No	*Award*	*Year*	*Operation*	*Total*
1.	Kirtii Chakra	1995	OP RAKSHAK J&K	01
2.	Shaurya Chakra	1993-95	-do-	04
3.	Sena Medal	1979	Field J&K	01
4.	Sena Medal	1993-96	Op Rakshak J&K	14
5.	COAS Commendation Cards	1962-71	NEFA & J&k	03
6.		1992-95	Op RAKSHAK (J&K)	22
7.	GOC-in-C Eastern Command Commendation Cards	1983	Op Garam Hawa	02

Serial No	Award	Year	Operation	Total
8.	GOC-in C Central Command Commendation Cards	1992	Op Rakshak (Pb)	02
9.	GOC-in –C Northern Command Commendation Cards	1992-95	Op Rakshak J&K	44
10.	VSM	1983	Op Garam Hawa	01
11.		1994	Op Rakshak J&K	01

DETAILS OF AWARDEES IN OP RAKSHAK J&K 1992-95

1.	13742820 A Lance/ Havildar Nek Singh (P)	Kirti Chakra
2.	IC-50927X Captain Hardeep Singh,SM	Shaurya Chakra
3.	13742820 A Lance/Havildar Nek Singh	Shaurya Chakra
4.	13743718K Lance/Naik Naresh Kumar(P)	Shaurya Chakra
5.	13751542Y Lance/Naik Rajeshwar Singh(P)	Shaurya Chakra
6.	IC-44759F Major Mahendra Jogdand	Sena Medal
7.	SS-33605F Major Avtar Singh	Sena Medal
8.	IC-49905M Major Lakhbinder Singh	Sena Medal
9.	IC-50927X Captain Hardeep Singh	Sena Medal
10.	MR-0631P Captain Amit Chatterjee	Sena Medal
11.	IC-51808N Captain Vinay Shahi	Sena Medal
12.	JC-192714A Subedar Bir Bahadur Chand	Sena Medal
13.	13738264X Havildar Lekh Raj	Sena Medal
14.	13739843W Havildar Tank Bahadur Chand	Sena Medal
15.	13742393 Naik Pawan Kumar	Sena Medal
16.	13750096 Lance/Naik Sudhir Kumar Thapa	Sena Medal
17.	1375201A Rifleman Roshan Singh	Sena Medal
18.	13748518X Rifleman Joginder Kumar (P)	Sena Medal
19.	12750862F Rifleman Phula Sherpa	Sena Medal
	VASHIST SEWA MEDAL	
20.	IC-27264L Colonel AC Soneja	VSM

CHIEF OF ARMY STAFF COMMENDATION CARDS

1.	IC-34402K	Lt	Colonel Ghanshyam Singh Katoch
2.	IC-39725W	Major	R C Katoch
3.	SS-33605F	Major	Avtar Singh
4.	IC-49905M	Major	Lakhbinder Singh, SM
5.	SS-35181P	Captain	Gulshan Chadha
6.	IC-51484N	2/Lt	Ashish Maini
7.	IC-35537X	2/Lt	Ashutosh Tripathi
8.	IC-52384P	2/Lt	R R Tiwari
9.	JC-167511L	Subedar	Ram Lal
10.	JC-192714A	Naib Sub	Bir Bahadur Chand
11.	JC 193839X	Subedar	Lekhraj
12.	13743357W	Havildar	Janesh Kumar Shahi
13.	13745180N	Havildar	Deepak Shahi
14.	13738806N	Havildar	Ghasita Ram
15.	13742392P	Naik	Pawan Kumar
16.	13742812F	Naik	Arjun Singh
17.	13744261A	L/Naik	Gurbachan Singh
18.	13748495F	Rifleman	Dev Raj
19.	13748507L	Rifleman	Mohan Lal
20.	13745984F	Rifleman	Naresh Kumar Thapa
21.	13750034X	Rifleman	Vir Bahadur
22.	13739186	L/Havildar	Surinder Kumar

AWARD OF GOC-IN-C NORTHERN COMMAND COMMENDATION CARD

1.	IC-33802K	Major	Harbans Singh Gill
2.	IC-33802K	Major	Harbans Singh Gill
3.	IC-37802F	Major	Harsh Kumar Tiwari, SM
4.	IC-37802F	Major	Harsh Kumar Tiwari, SM
5.	IC-49905M	Captain	LakhbinderSingh, SM
6.	IC-50927X	Captain	Hardeep Singh Sohi, SM
7.	IC-51808N	Captain	Vinay Shahi, SM
8.	JC-175114F	Subedar	Ganesh Bahadur
9.	JC-183527A	Subedar	Babbar Jung
10.	JC-193893X	Subedar	Lekh Raj

11.	JC-193893X	Subedar	Lekh Raj
12.	JC-185202A	Subedar	Omkar Singh Manhas (P)
13.	JC-205717P	Subedar	Roshan Lal
14.	JC-178105L	Subedar	Rajinder Singh
15.	JC-578286P	Naib Subedar	Onkar Chand Rana
16.	13741985N	Havildar	Dharmender
17.	13743221M	Havildar	Shamsher Singh
18.	13738102M	Coy Havildar	Major Satpal Singh
19.	13744173K	Havildar	Jit Bahadur Chhetri
20.	13745380H	Havildar	Deepak Shahi
21.	13742411K	Havildar	Jaswant Singh
22.	13741673K	Havildar	Surjeet Singh
23.	13743724H	Havildar	Rachhpal Singh
24.	13738204L	Havildar	Lekh Raj
25.	13743081L	Naik	Subhash Singh
26.	13743350F	Naik	Raj Mohan
27.	13747324H	Lance/Naik	Kartar Nath
28.	13742531Y	Lance/Naik	Diley Ram
29.	13742820A	Lance/Naik	Nek Singh
30.	13750862F	Rifleman	Phula Sherpa
31.	13751669M	Rifleman	Sanjeev Kumar Pradhan
32.	13752406P	Rifleman	Chetan Singh
33.	13751562M	Rifleman	Hukam Singh
34.	13750652F	Lance/Naik	Mess wtr Sahdev Pal
35.	13751134N	Rifleman	Ishwar Singh
36.	13754814 Y	Rifleman	Sher Bahadur Thapa
37.	13751526 F	Rifleman	Chandra Bahadur
38.	13743651W	Lance/Naik (TS)	Rattan Chand
39.	13749361M	Rifleman	Bipat Kumar
40.	13750761M	Rifleman	Damar Bahadur
41.	13751988N	Rifleman	Ran Bahadur Rai
42.	13751585N	Rifleman	Lekhram
43.	13751524F	Rifleman	Raj Singh
44.	13751557F	Rifleman	Bhagirath

RECOVERY OF WARLIKE STORES IN OP RAKSHAK (J&K)

1.	Rifles AK-47/56/72/75	187
2.	General Purpose Machine Gun (GPMG) with Box Magazines	2
3.	Universal Machine Gun (UMG)	4
4.	RPG Launcher	3
5.	Snipper Rifle	1
6.	Pistols/Revolvers	50
7.	Shot Guns	9
8.	Radio Sets	12
9.	Magazines AK Rifles	533
10.	Magazines Pistol	56
11.	Ammunition AK Rifles	11592
12.	Ammunition (UMG)	298
13.	Ammunition Belted (UMG)	252
14.	Ammunition Sniper Rifle	250
15.	Ammunition for SLR	42
16.	2″ Mor HE Bomb	1
17.	Rockets RPG 7V	7
18.	Ammunition Pistol	547
19.	Grenades All Types	119
20.	Electrical Detonaters	128
21.	PEAK	1.350 Kg
22.	Other Explosives	12 Kg
23.	Fuze Wire	319 Kg
24.	Gelatine Sticks	22
25.	Compass	1
26.	Binocular	4
27.	A/Per Mine	1
28.	Clay More Mine	1
29.	Improvised Explosives Devices	20
30.	IED Exploder	1
31.	Gun Powder	16 Kgs
32.	Night Vision Device	1

BIBLIOGRAPHY

Adarsh Sein Anand, 'Development of Constitution of Jammu & Kashmir' (New DelhiLight & Life Publishers 1980).

A G Noorani, The Kashmir Dispute1947-2012(Tulika Books 35A/5 Shahpur Jat New Delhi 110049 India).

Bakshi, G D, 'Warriers of Sun And Snow', Jammu and Kashmir Rifles, Vanity Books Delhi 2006.

Balraj Puri, Kashmir Towards Insurgency (Orient Longwan 1993, Hyderabad).

Bhim Singh, Flames in Kashmir, Har Anand Publications Pvt Ltd 364-A Chirag Delhi, New Delhi 110017.

Bourke-White Margret, 'Half Way to Freedom' (New York Simon and Schuster, 1949).

Brocher Michael, 'The Strugle for Kashmir' (New York Oxford University Press New York 1953).

Chopra V D, Genesis of Indo-Pakistan Conflict on Kashmir (New Delhi Patriot Publications 1990).

Dr Sudhir Bloeria, IAS, Pakistan's Insurgency vs India's Security Manas Publications New Delhi 110002 (India).

Dr Sudhir Bloeria, IAS, He Battle of Zojila, 1948 Har Anand Publications, New Delhi 1996.

Daruwala, K N, Pakistan occupied Kashmir, South Asian Centre for Strategic studies, New Delhi 1996

Jagmohan, My Frozen Turbulance in Kashmir, Allied Publications New Delhi, 1991.

J K Sharma, Kashmir in Blood Tears, (Bookwell New Delhi).

Karim Maj Gen (Retd), Afsir Kashmir the Troubled Frontiers, Lancer Publications, New Delhi 1994.

K Kuldip Singh, Brig, 'Kurukshetra to Kargil', Lancer Publications, New Delhi 110016

Munshi D N, Agony of Kashmir' (Delhi Sureshi Prakashan 1992).

Mamta Rajawat, "Kashmir Shadow of Terrorism" Anmol Publication Pvt Ltd New Delhi 110002 (India).

Prasad S N and Dharm Pal, History of Operations in Jammu and Kashmir (1947-48) MOD New Delhi 1987.

S K Sharma and Usha Sharma, 'Kashmir and the World', Deep and Deep Publications, Rajouri Garden New Delhi 110027.

S P Sinha, VSM, Brig (Dr), 'Forever in Operations' Volume II, Published by General Staff Branch, Headquarters 8 Mountain Division, Printed by Headquarters Delhi Area, Delhi Cantt.

Y M Bammi, Lt Gen, 'War Against Insurgency & Terrorism in Kashmir' (Natraj Publishers. Dehradun, India).

Regimental Magzines

DURJEYA, Regimental magazine 1993 edition.

DURJEYA, Regimental magazine 1994 edition.

DURJEYA, Regimental magazine 1995 edition.

DURJEYA, Regimental magazine 1996 edition.

Newspapers

Kashmir Times, 8 October 1993, Vol 44, No 279, No JM 5.

Kashmir Times, 22 May 1993, Vol 44, No 140, Regd No JM 5.

Greater Kashmir, 3 January 1995, Vol 8, No 2, 30 RAJAB-UL-MURAJAB AH Srinagar.

Greater Kashmir, 11 March 1995, Vol 8, No 31, 9 SHAWAL 1415 AH Srinagar.

Greater Kashmir, 21 August 1994, Vol 7, No 186, 12 RABI-UL-AWAL 1415 AH Srinagar.

Francois Gautier, The Ferangi's column, pages 20-23. Reproduced, Har Anand Publications 2001, A western journalist's account of operations in India(reproduced).